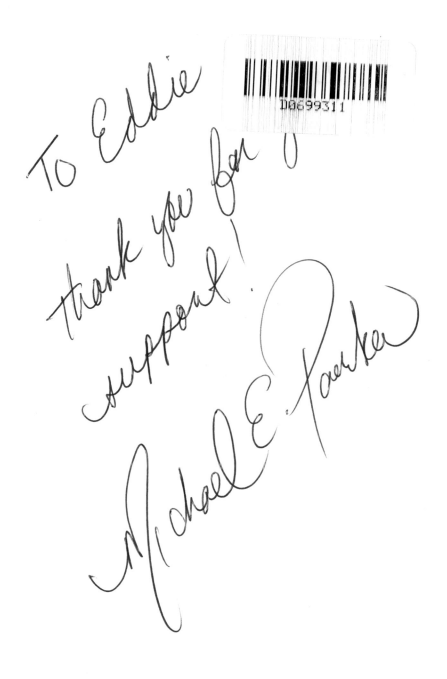

WHO SAID SO?

*The Questions Revolutionary
Businesses Ask That
Make Them Successful*

MICHAEL D. PARKER

John Wiley & Sons, Inc.

Published by John Wiley & Sons, Inc., Hoboken, New Jersey.
Published simultaneously in Canada.

For general information on our other products and services or for technical support, please contact our Customer Care Department within the United States at (800) 762-2974, outside the United States at (317) 572-3993 or fax (317) 572-4002.

Wiley also publishes its books in a variety of electronic formats. Some content that appears in print may not be available in electronic books. For more information about Wiley products, visit our web site at www.wiley.com.

Library of Congress Cataloging-in-Publication Data:

Parker, Michael, 1975–
    Who said so? : the questions revolutionary businesses ask that make them successful / Michael Parker.
        p. cm.
    ISBN 978-0-470-21280-6 (cloth)
    1. Success in business. 2. Customer relations—Management.
    3. Management. I. Title.
    HF5386.P255   2008
    658.4'01—dc22
                                                        2007032139

Printed in the United States of America.

10 9 8 7 6 5 4 3 2 1

CONTENTS

FOREWORD

I became part of the Toyota manufacturing family after 18 years in the U.S. automotive industry and was excited to be exposed to an entirely different way of thinking that would change my career forever. I personally was involved in helping lead the implementation of the Toyota Production System at NUMMI—the joint venture between Toyota and General Motors— where I witnessed a new way of thinking enter and reshape an industry because of its power and business truth. In this book, Mr. Michael E. Parker explains a management approach that simplifies the treasures of the Toyota Production System and management philosophy, while at the same time provides a fresh look at what true business is all about: the customer.

In *Who Said So?* Mr. Parker introduces readers to a management approach—Value-Centered Management—that succeeds in translating the successes of the Toyota Production System and management philosophy in a way that can be incorporated into any industry or business environment. It is a delightful book filled with great leadership insights and universal management practices that can be quickly and easily understood.

The uniqueness of Mr. Parker's work is that the lessons, tools, and methods are expressed simply and concisely through an enjoyable story of the relationship between a son and his father. The son is formally educated but struggling with real-life management and leadership issues that are difficult to learn from management books alone. His father is a street-smart man who, through long experience and hard knocks, has developed a keen sense of management practices that really work. Seeing how their shaky past relationship improves and strengthens is very heartwarming, as the father displays a rare ability to pass the value of his experiences on to his son.

As background, Michael and I were colleagues at NUMMI, located in the Bay Area of northern California. He was one of the brightest and hardest-working young leaders we hired into the Production Control organization. Michael quickly gained a firm understanding of the Toyota Production System through the many challenging assignments he was handed.

Michael has loaded *Who Said So?* with Toyota's leadership philosophies, management practices, tools, and universally applicable ideas. But he's kept it a quick and easy read. In fact, I challenge you not to get caught up in the story or be fascinated with the important messages delivered throughout the book. And I encourage you to highlight or underline the many useful management practices you'll find.

As an established executive, I have read many books that claim to unleash great secrets of business management and business success; however, this book truly delivers. As you'll see, this will not be another management book gathering dust on the shelf but, instead, a quick and ready reference to scan and refresh your thinking on a regular basis. I'm sure you will enjoy it.

GARY CONVIS
Executive Vice President
Toyota Engineering and Manufacturing
Managing Officer, Toyota Motor Corporation

ACKNOWLEDGMENTS

A rriving at the end of this book is an overwhelming experience, but even more overwhelming is my appreciation for the people and experiences that prepared me to complete this project.

First, I wish to acknowledge those who opened doors for me and taught me great lessons throughout my career at NUMMI (the joint venture between Toyota and General Motors). Thanks to:

- Bruce Hoyt, who created the first opportunity for me at NUMMI. Without Bruce, I never would have met the wonderful people I acknowledge next.

- Gary Convis and Akio Toyoda, for their overwhelming support and example throughout the many projects I was given at NUMMI. They may have not noticed, but I was forever watching and gleaning from their effective leadership approaches. It was an honor to be at NUMMI with Akio Toyoda (the grandson of Toyota's founder) and to work on a project he had such a strong interest in. Thank you for everything, Toyoda-san. And thank you Gary Convis for your support and example. You embody the word "leadership."

- Kant (KC) Hung, who was the most supportive manager I had at NUMMI. KC, I appreciate you for giving me so many opportunities and for seeing what I truly had on the inside. I appreciate you for giving me the flexibility to grow and for listening when I needed to talk or needed direction.

- All of the individuals who supported my learning of the Toyota Production System directly from Toyota Motor Corporation (TMC) in Japan: Kurt Onoue for being such a great teacher of the Toyota Production System and taking the time to impart so much knowledge to me. You became a true friend and always supported my growth and development. Yasuharo Tanaka and Kats Nishimoto for instructing me in the great depths of Toyota Internal and External Logistics, and Systems Development Kaizen. It was a great pleasure traveling across the country with you and learning from such a wonderful team. From the stops at Dunkin' Donuts in the early morning, to always reminding me to go to the actual work site (Genchi Genbutsu, you would say) to see what was really happening (even in the blistering cold at the consolidation centers in Chicago and Detroit). You made me a better professional and taught me about the Toyota Production System the right way. Toshi Tsutsumi, if it was not for your superior interpreting skills much of my learning potential would never have been realized. I highly value our relationship and thank you for all your support during the intense projects.

- George Summerville, the first true friend I met at NUMMI. Thank you for taking the time to get to know me when I first came to NUMMI and for remaining an outstanding friend throughout my stay. You have continued to be a brother to me.

- All of the team members and colleagues I worked with at NUMMI, TLSI, Ryder, TMS, TMMNA, and TMC throughout the United States, Canada, and Japan.

Second, I feel blessed today to have the best team in the world and want to acknowledge them. I am honored to be affiliated with such a wonderful team at all of my companies: Stellar Enterprise, Jovance Beauty & Wellness, Stalaro's Boutique, Star Team Investments, Star Team Property Management, Value-Centered Management Institute, Lifeskills 411, and the "You Are a CEO" Program.

I would like to thank those team members who despite all odds, opposition, and great challenges, stood with me in the more difficult times of my career. My respect for you cannot be measured, and I realize that we would not be where we are today if it was not for you. I will never forget your labor of love and the show of unity that you continue to display to assist me in building something for a higher purpose. You share my belief that it is not just about being successful, but about getting there the right way and for the right reasons. I appreciate you all.

At this time, I would like to acknowledge several key team members for their overwhelming support and sacrifice: Nancy Wallace, Cynthia Green, Elealeh Smith, Bella Survine, Darral Brown, Darrell Booker, Megan Tomasello, Terry Fulton, Rita Johnson, Maya Parker, Carrie Fulton, Clifton Byrd, Adrienne Clark, Teresa Long, Marcus Smith, Harold Cordier, Alisa Brown, Sharmayne Thompson, Nick Viera, Julie Parker, Mallase Luckett, Charlene Ciruso, Lashanna Jackson, Shawn Smith, Sahaja Pitre, Elijah Smith, St. Clair Davis, Kiesha Pinel, Daniel Smith, Amanda Thomas, Elijah Steward, Greta Butler, and Ray and Valentina Anderson.

I would like to thank all of our shareholders and investors. Without their contributions and support none of my entrepreneurship journey would have been possible. I especially thank those who gave because they truly believed in me and my vision without doubt, without fear, and without complaint. You are special, and I appreciate you and will never forget you. Of course, I would also like to thank our professional legal and accounting team for being there for us through thick and thin. As a result, I would like to thank Steven Bangerter, Tom Thomas, Bill Frazier, and the wonderful staff from the law offices of Steven R. Bangerter. In addition, I would like to thank Elaine Kawasaki, Ed Cagawan, and the wonderful staff of Timpson Garcia, LLP.

Third, I would like to thank those who greatly assisted me in putting this book together. We have completed a book to be proud of, and I am thankful for the lessons learned. This is a beginning that will continue into an exciting future in which volumes of valuable information will be shared. Below I would like to acknowledge and thank a few individuals who made it all possible:

- Adrian Gostick for assisting me in writing this book and leading me to such a wonderful publishing company, John Wiley & Sons. Adrian, you are a great listener and your writing talent is impeccable. I have learned many things from you and look forward to working on many projects together in the future. You are the best!

- The professionals at John Wiley & Sons for all of their support, especially Laurie Harting for assisting me in bringing everything together in a way that will make the book more successful. I appreciate your honesty and candidness, which allowed me to understand many great truths of the publishing world. Most importantly you helped me see things from the customer's perspective. Special thanks to Christine Kim for her support with respect to coordinating marketing activities and to Jessica Langan-Peck, Kate Lindsay and Shannon Vargo for their overall support.

- Elealeh Smith for coordinating all of the artwork for the book and for being my right hand with regard to all of the Value-Centered Management and Lean Management methodologies that I have been teaching through the years. Your ability to help others understand what is in my mind is remarkable, and you have made my job so much easier through your undeniable talent. Elealeh, you are the Lean Queen!

- Jimmy L. Williams and Mathew Acosta for creating the artwork featured in the book. Thank you for allowing me to use your talent to showcase this concept. I wish you both success and would love to work together again.

- Bella Survine (the greatest executive assistant of all time) for assisting me in keeping my sanity every day and throughout this project. Without you, I wouldn't get anything done. Somehow you keep up with me and do it with such cheerfulness and without complaint. Bell, I truly appreciate you!

Finally, I give special acknowledgment to my God, who makes all things possible; and to my friends, godparents, and my beautiful wife. Thanks to:

- Many true friends throughout the Body of Christ who love and support me. Especially those who live in Albuquerque, New Mexico; Vallejo, California; Union City, California; Moreno Valley, California; Baton Rouge, Louisiana; Tyler, Texas; and in North Carolina. You know who you are. If a person finds just one true friend in a lifetime they should consider themselves extremely privileged;

however, I am grateful to have so many of these friends support me with pure hearts. They stood with me in days of prosperity and days of adversity. I love you and appreciate you.

- Lacy Hawkins and the late Etta Hawkins for being the true parents I never had. You saved my life, and as a result I am where I am today. I hope that you see your sacrifice was not in vain. As I continue to grow in my career, I will never forget who I am and how much both of you mean to me. I love you, forever.

- My wife and friend, Maya Parker. Without your support, patience, and understanding, I could not have accomplished any of this. We were married as I was embarking on this journey of Value-Centered Management. Over the last eight years you have been a great strength and an example to me, even though you may not always realize it. I cannot tell you how much I appreciate your friendship and your honesty, and you will always have a very special place in my heart. I love you, Maya.

A quick note after everything else: I appreciate all those who supported me and didn't support me, who built me up and who tried to tear me down, who were honest with me and who talked behind my back, who stuck with me in times of challenge and those who fled. All of you made me stronger and taught me something that only life's experiences can. Through the good and the bad, the laughter and the tears, I have never forgotten the wisdom from the scriptures:

And we know that all things work together for good to them that love God, to them who are the called according to his purpose. (Romans 8:28)

INTRODUCTION

At Toyota in the 1990s, I was fascinated with what made operations work. The thought of several processes and groups of people all working together to accomplish a goal sparked my attention and curiosity, but not for the first time.

I had grown up in the rough neighborhoods of Richmond, California, trying to avoid the evils of the inner city. Since I was often alone, I had plenty of time to think, and plenty of time to learn about human nature. Thankfully, I focused a lot of my teenage energy on studying people and dreaming of how they could work together.

Eventually I found my way to Cal State University Hayward, where I studied purchasing and operations and then earned an MBA. Finally, I was ready to tackle the corporate world. A post with Toyota was my first journey toward understanding lean management. It opened my mind to this brilliant approach to production efficiency. While working there, I ended up in Japan on special assignment at the same time as Akio Toyoda, the grandson of the auto giant's founder. He and other leaders noticed me in a presentation and selected me to be on a team that would implement lean manufacturing principles throughout North America. I was on a fast track and had a chance to work with many brilliant executives and team members.

Even with the amazing opportunity in arguably the world's strongest manufacturing environment, I wasn't satisfied. Along the way I had developed a love of the service industry, and I had a feeling that what I was learning about lean manufacturing could be applied there. From what I could see, few service organizations were working anywhere nearly as efficiently or with as much consistent customer focus as they could. And so, during my years at Toyota, I spent lunches and breaks grilling lean experts from Japan on how these principles might be applied outside of manufacturing. They admitted the concepts could work, but had never thought of implementing them that way. I brainstormed about using lean in a kitchen, in consulting work, in processing mortgage loans, and in a dozen other applications. At night, I began to think about starting an organization that could use these principles in a manufacturing and service industry setting.

Years ago, Kirchiro Toyoda, Taichi Ohno and those who developed lean manufacturing had come to America to study business processes. Legends claim they visited giant grocery stores, manufacturing plants, warehouses, and anyplace where processes could be found. Everywhere they went, they learned. And they took back what they found to Japan where they worked with it, molded it, and eventually created a philosophy that would change the way most of the world builds products. For me, the experience at Toyota was a similar beginning.

Lean management principles taught me to get rid of waste and improve processes. And yet I wanted to make the principles my own, as well as add the component of a stringent focus on value and a value-centered culture. So in 2001, I went out on my own to show what the concepts might do outside of manufacturing. Founding Stellar Enterprise, I began to employ my own approach to business that I call Value-Centered Management. It is a philosophy that looks at every part of a business, helping managers and team members understand how to truly serve the customer—from the founding philosophies and approach to business, to determining the tangible structure, process and approach that will get the best results.

Together with an outstanding leadership team, we have created seven subsidiaries that employ a host of vibrant team members—many of whom were touched by one of my favorite companies—lifeskills 411™. The lifeskills program has affected the lives of youth and adults throughout the nation, most especially in Northern California and is near and dear to my heart (but is a story for another day). I'm honored to say that our companies are now thriving and have been growing at an annual average rate of 25 percent per year over those six years. In addition, at 90-plus percent ratings, our customer satisfaction levels are near the top of each of their respective industries.

With our small successes we have begun taking our message to others. Today, our Value-Centered Management Institute teaches businesses and people to build stronger organizations that serve real customer needs and unleash team members to achieve all they can. In short, we help create lean organizations centered around what the customer values. And when you think about it, that's what all business should be about. For too long we have accepted traditional wisdom taught in business schools and by many leaders of our organizations. We have followed because their wisdom produced acceptable results. But who said acceptable is good enough? Who says we can't achieve more? Successful businesses are not run on tradition anymore. Their leaders are tuning into the spoken and unspoken desires of their customers and are building organizations and team members that focus on value in every aspect of their delivery.

And we have found that anyone can learn how to take these principles and apply them in their work lives—whether they run a consulting firm or manage a team in a multinational company. We have applied Value-Centered Management in retail, service, financial, manufacturing, technical, and other industries, and the results are consistent and remarkable.

After all, if you know what your customers want and deliver it day by day, how can you fail?

MICHAEL E. PARKER

CHAPTER 1

Is This as Good as It Gets?

The Broken Link between Success and the Status Quo

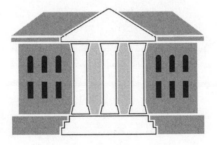

Sitting at his kitchen table, surrounded by the management books that had always made him feel safe, John felt the hair rise on the back of his neck.

Until now, he hadn't paid much attention to the B-grade horror flick playing on late-night television on the counter. It was on for background noise, to keep him company as he read. Now, with all his senses on red alert, John was acutely aware of how the actor's hands shook as he pushed open the door of the deserted house and took a tentative step inside.

There was something frighteningly familiar about the scene, John realized. But he couldn't put his finger on it. Suddenly, behind the actor, something moved in the darkness, and John's stomach lurched: *That guy on the screen,* he thought, *that's me.*

Annoyed with himself, John snapped off the set and tossed his takeout box into the trash. But, sitting alone in the quiet, he couldn't stop the thoughts filling his mind. *That's me. Going in where everyone else has failed, thinking I can save the day.*

John rubbed his eyes. He hadn't been sleeping well lately, with his mind all wrapped up in his job, and he was tired.

"Time to call it a night," he said out loud to no one. He flipped off the kitchen light and crossed the adjoining living room, pausing for a moment to admire the painting that dwarfed the small room: an enormous abstract artwork consisting of overlapping shades of blue. He'd bought it with his AXD Solutions signing bonus. It was much too big for his apartment; John had known that from the beginning. However, there was something about the undulating current of the piece that reminded him of a fast-flowing river. It radiated the energy that he had felt that day. Sometimes, when he studied it, he still felt enveloped, surrounded by millions of droplets of water flowing rapidly toward the same destination. But not tonight. Tonight, it just made him feel like he was drowning.

The thing was, his job—the one that he had dreamed of, the one that was the envy of all his college friends—was driving him insane. Of course, it hadn't always been this way. His enthusiasm and success in graduate school had attracted attention early on. He hadn't even completed his MBA program when AXD Solutions, an eight-hundred-pound gorilla in the IT industry, came looking for him. Suddenly, he'd found himself on the fast track without even putting together a resume. His immediate and phenomenal success with Trenneth, his first client, had confirmed his status as the heir apparent within AXD.

During John's heady first six months with AXD, his dad, Tim, had been the only person with any reservations about the certainty of a very bright future for John. Tim had been a midlevel executive with a major airline for more than 20 years. Although he was proud of John's quick success, his experiences in the corporate world made him concerned. Tim had worked his way up through his company without the benefit of a degree, and the long hours and stress of his career had been hard on his psyche.

Once, when John was still a teenager at home, he had run in from a pickup game of basketball to find his dad fingering a new line on the wall where his parents marked their children's heights in permanent marker. The line was just about his dad's height. "Just checking to see how I'm measuring up, you know, if I've shrunk any," his father had joked. It wasn't until just recently that John had realized he might have been talking about his own fading career ambitions.

Looking back now, there were many signs through the years that his dad was discouraged by his job. Still, John had chosen to follow his father's footsteps into the corporate world.

I walked into the situation with my eyes wide open, John thought to himself. *Or did I?*

His phenomenal success with Trenneth had been followed by several projects where John had turned in solid but decidedly less-impressive performances. It was on his three-year anniversary with the company that John had first realized that his star was already fading. Somehow, somewhere along the way, he had lost the passion and was worried his work was sliding into mediocrity. In desperation, during his most recent project, he'd turned to his old college textbooks, studying late into the night in search of what was missing.

What was he missing? John's eyes scanned the surface of the painting, as if searching for an answer, but he soon found he was too tired to rehash it all tonight. His mind jogged erratically back to the horror movie. *Why don't the guys in these movies ever turn on the lights?* he asked himself. Now, that was an easier question. *Maybe because they're afraid of what they'll see.*

John froze. The thought was unexpected and jarring—and seemed to somehow imply something unflattering about his personal situation. Rather than deal with it, he hit the wall switch and the living room went dark.

"Pardon me," the woman next to John bumped his chair as she settled into her seat. He'd been early; the first one at the one o'clock managers meeting; but now the room was filling up fast. Someone passed him an agenda.

John remembered how he used to love these meetings when he was on the Trenneth project; there were so many exciting things to report. Today, his turn to report would take maybe thirty seconds, max. His small development team was holding its own. Right on schedule. Nothing to be ashamed of, yet he was embarrassed. He hated that there was nothing spectacular happening with his group. On the upside, he could pretty much zone out during the meeting. As usual, the pressure would be on the managers whose projects were in trouble.

He scanned the report. Cheryl was up first. Her team was at least a month behind on the Mentec project, and there were red dots all over her Gantt chart, not good. He scanned the faces around the table. Dave. Jay. Brent. Andrew. Michelle. Phil. But no Cheryl. *I'd be hiding out, too,* thought John. *No, no I wouldn't,* he corrected himself. *I'd be killing myself to get that software out the door.*

John was still lost in thought when Kaye, the regional vice president, came into the room at a calculated ten minutes past the hour. When John looked up, she caught his eye and greeted him personally, although he was seated four seats down from her.

"Hi, John. Glad to see your projects are on schedule. I hear good things about you," she said, talking over the heads of several other managers.

It was a compliment, but he felt his guts freeze up momentarily. Who had been saying good things? His clients? Had she spoken with his clients? Usually she only did that once a year, just before performance appraisals, and that was via a written survey. What was up?

"We won't wait for Cheryl. But there are some problems in her area," Kaye addressed the group. "We're 640 man hours behind schedule on Mentec's deliverable. The deadline is in 90 days and we've got to punch production up to meet it. I've heard there have been some problems with sales adding additional requirements that have slowed the development cycle. Mike, can you give me sales' perspective?"

At the question, everyone's eyes took on a faraway look. Some stared down at the agenda in a vague sort of way. They all knew this could take a while. Mentally, John tried to track the conversation, although it was hard. It was after lunch, and he'd heard it all a million times before. The blame game was on.

Blah, blah, blah, blah. Something about the customer constantly changing the target. Blah, blah, blah. The customer is completely unreasonable. Yada, yada, yada. They say what we're creating isn't what they pictured and described. Blah, blah, blah, blah. The programmers can't seem to get it right. Blah, blah. Blah, blah. More complaints about the programmers. Something, something, something. Maybe we should turn it over to a new project manager. Blah, blah, blah.

Wait!

John looked around, startled. Had he said that out loud? Apparently not. No one was reacting. Next to him, Dave continued slowly filling the margins of his progress report with spirals . . . and rather gruesome skulls and tombstones. Was everyone in the room mentally checked out? Hadn't they heard that last part?

For the rest of the meeting, John was acutely aware of what was said. The first round of the blame game was declared a tie and the topic was tabled after a 35-minute tangent into the pros and cons of outsourcing to programmers in India. Round two centered around the declining sales of an internally produced accounting software product. All this was followed by a cursory discussion about upcoming HR open enrollment featuring reductions in PTO benefits, the summer party in August at a local amusement park, and some efficiency training. And then it was over. John looked at his watch. They had finished in just under two hours—a miracle! Managers meetings sometimes ran until dark.

As he pushed his seat back, Kaye called to him. "John, I'd like to meet with you in my office in ten minutes. Are you free?"

The VP's office was bright, full of brushed aluminum wall panels and uncomfortable, modern armchairs. It was the kind of place John pictured himself occupying someday. As she wrapped up a phone call, John calmed his nerves by visualizing how his painting of blue currents would look on the wall next to her desk.

On the phone, Kaye watched him as his eyes scanned the room, the one it had taken her years to earn. *Cool your jets, kiddo,* she thought, as the vendor on the phone launched into his best pitch. *You have to pay your dues—and then wait for me to move up into a corner office on the fourth floor.* She smiled. John grinned back.

Hanging up, Kaye excused herself for a moment to talk to her assistant. When she came back, she sat behind her desk instead of taking the chair next to John. *Remind him who's boss,* she thought.

"It's been a good couple of years for you," Kaye began. "First Trenneth, then AmSen. Both solid deliveries. Now Sun Disk and TCG are going well." She leaned back in her chair and flicked her pen lightly on the side of her leather chair. "People are talking about the fast track and you being the next Blaine Mukai." As she said it, her eyes searched his face.

John hardly knew how to respond. The words were positive. But, somehow, the way she said it didn't come across that way.

What could he say? He shifted in his chair. "Well, I—"

"Here's the deal," Kaye interrupted. "Cheryl has left the company. Not voluntarily. You heard about the problems with Mentec. They're ready to go with another vendor. That's how bad it's gotten."

"But we haven't missed the drop-dead date," said John. "We've suffered a few setbacks, and they're packing their bags?"

Kaye continued. "The delays have them nervous, sure, but it's more than that. They say we aren't responsive to their needs. They didn't work well with Cheryl."

"We—the CEO and COO were in on this one—want you to take over the account," she said. "They are impressed by your talent, creativity, and energy. 'Youthful energy,' were their exact words, I think. We need someone who's fearless—willing to take on a wide breadth of problems and drive results. We can't afford to lose this client. You're the guy."

John was speechless. Six months ago, he would have been salivating over this kind of project, a chance to showcase what he really could do. Now, he wasn't so sure. There was a metallic taste in his mouth, a symptom of the adrenaline now surging through his system. *So, what's it going to be? Fight or flight?* he asked himself.

"Okay. What about Sun Disk and TCG?"

"Small-time stuff. We'll have someone else finish your other projects. Mentec is huge for us."

"Okay." He paused and rubbed his hand through his hair. "Tell me where to start."

"I knew you'd be up to the challenge," she said, "so I had my assistant put this packet together for you. It'll bring you up to date. We've got four people on this project. Ray Edvik, your senior consultant, can walk you through things. You know Ray; he's in the cube bank next to your team. Get started, then we can meet back here in a few days to discuss any questions you've come up with."

She stood to shake his hand and walked him to the door. Returning to her desk, Kaye wondered if she'd done the right thing. *For the sake of the company—oh, let's be honest, for the sake of my own career—I need him to succeed. But not too well. I know what happens to young executives who experience wild success: They replace regional vice presidents like me.*

The next day was a blur. John said goodbye to his trusted team members and introduced himself to a new group of four relative strangers: Ray Edvik, a senior guy with ten-plus years under his belt put in at several firms (John didn't recall ever meeting him before); Blake, a seven-year veteran; Kiki, a junior programmer with a couple of years experience, all at AXD Solutions; and Todd, the graphics guy.

Putting everyone on autopilot for the moment, John immersed himself in the Mentec project. Using reports and memos, John traced the slow decline of Cheryl's group from confident enthusiasm, through hopeful rewrites, and, finally, to the last client conference call, which, by all accounts, had been a train wreck. Mike, AXD's sales director, laid it out for him in gruesome detail when John ran into him in the hallway on Tuesday.

"So, after three hours on a conference call going nowhere, Cheryl finally tells Mentec that we aren't going to make any more changes, period," Mike had told John in whispers during the impromptu hallway meeting. "She says legally we're in compliance with the original contract, and that's it."

Although John hadn't said a word, Mike must have read something in his face. Mike ran his hand across his bald head and sighed. "All I can say is, hey, look, we've got people here who can sell ice to Eskimos, but none of them can figure Mentec out. Even my best people can't make any headway."

By Wednesday, John had come to two conclusions: The product not only appeared to meet every one of the customer's specifications but surpass them, and, for some indefinable reason, Mentec hated it.

There's got to be a way to do this, John thought to himself for the millionth time. *We've got to get into the heads of the people at Mentec and figure out—*

The thought was interrupted by a knock at his office door.

"Got a moment?" Ray cracked the door and poked his head around. He was a big man in his late forties, who (so far, anyway) wore a different-colored Polo golf shirt to work every day, always with dark blue khakis.

"Just wanted to see if you have any questions so far on the project. Kiki's code can be a little rough. I have to nurse her along a little sometimes. She's still getting the hang of it all."

John hadn't noticed any quality differences in their work, but it made him question Kiki's abilities: *What were Kiki's skills? Was part of the delay caused by Ray having to cover for her?*

Long after Ray had left his office, John was still wondering about his people. His thoughts were disturbed by a loud growl; his stomach was complaining. He glanced down at his watch; It was two o'clock. He needed to take a break. *What had Stephanie said her day would be like today?* He tried to remember. As a busy event planner, his girlfriend's schedule was even more nuts than his. He speed-dialed his number one.

"Hey, Steph, want to grab a late lunch? We can get some Thai."

Thirty minutes later, sitting in the bright and ornate surroundings of their favorite restaurant, John looked over at Stephanie and felt himself relax a little. She smiled, waiting for him to fill her in on the latest. They had been dating for about two years now, and the Thai Café was where they always came when things got a little out of control. It was their secret smoke signal for distress.

The place was perfect. Always busy, yet never frantic. The waitresses treated them like family, looking up and smiling whenever they arrived. It was corny, but John and Stephanie even had a favorite table tucked into a little alcove.

The waitress took their order and, as she walked away, Stephanie noticed three men in business suits passing their table.

"John," she said. "That man being seated, with the orange tie. Isn't he your client from Trenneth?" She had been introduced to Mr. Jackson at a corporate reception she'd attended with John a couple years ago, and she'd been struck by how well he and John had seemed to hit it off.

"It is!" John was already pushing back his chair. "Give me just one minute," he said, holding up a finger. "I want to say hello."

From the table she watched Mr. Jackson's surprise, followed by his obvious pleasure in seeing John again. He asked John something, and John shook his head, motioning her way. She waved and smiled. During a pause in the pleasant hum of conversation around her, she heard Jackson tell his companions loudly, "This is the guy who transformed warehousing for us." As John said goodbye, Jackson stood and shook John's hand with both of his.

John returned to the table with lifted spirits. The spicy food reenergized him. And Stephanie helped him to refocus. As they left the restaurant, Stephanie couldn't help but laugh at the magic of the place. As usual, a trip to the Thai Café had transformed them.

John got back to the office just minutes before his first staff meeting with his new group and was pleasantly surprised to find he was excitedly anticipating it. The team's war room, really just a table and some mismatched chairs in an open area, was located clear on the other side of the building, next to his group's printer. To get to it, you had to pass through a graveyard of several empty cubes, each with a broken chair and dusty old monitor. *Why don't we just get rid of all this junk?* he wondered.

He stopped on the way to the meeting to ask Ray to bring along a Gantt chart of part of the project— something that was missing from the documentation—so that the group could assess what came next. There were some parts of the project marked completed that hadn't made it to testing yet, and the flowchart of the project was sketchy at best.

Ray wasn't there; but he noticed Kiki in her cube, punching away at a keyboard. He poked his head into the cube.

"Hey, you coming to the meeting? I was hoping to get started in about three minutes."

She looked up and smiled. "Yeah, sure. I just had to reboot my computer. It froze up again."

Kiki got up and walked with John to the war room. She didn't say much as he made small talk about the weather, and he noticed that her knuckles, clutching a yellow legal pad, were white.

Ray was talking loudly as they joined the rest of the group already there. Ray was going on and on about parsing code. Todd might have been listening, but it was hard to tell. He was leaning back, with his long, lanky legs stretched out in front of him, staring at the ceiling with a frown. Blake was on a cell phone, one finger in his ear to block out Ray's booming voice. As John and Kiki sat down, he ended the call. All eyes locked in on the boss.

Well, might as well just dive right in, he thought.

"I don't know how much you know about what's happened over the past few days in response to Mentec's concerns, other than that Cheryl has left the company," John began. "Let's just start by saying that this is the group that will finish the project . . . on time and to specifications."

John had spent a lot of time formulating this first statement. He wanted to reassure the group that no one else was leaving, but also communicate the challenge at hand. It had the desired effect on Kiki. She smiled and visibly relaxed.

"I have some questions that I hope you can answer."

In short order, John had learned that no one on the staff had ever spoken with anyone at Mentec; that was Cheryl's job. They had never seen the overall project Gantt chart, either. No one was really sure what the next step was. And no one had any idea of their deadlines.

"Cheryl just gave us a new piece of the project as we finished something," offered Kiki apologetically.

John was particularly amazed to discover that, although everyone had known there were some problems, no one (except possibly Ray) had understood how extensive they were until Cheryl left.

"I calculate that we've spent roughly one month, that's 640 man hours, on rewrites," said John. "But we haven't fixed the problem yet? What's going on?"

"Look, these people are never happy," said Ray. "I built them a Porsche and they'd rather have a go-kart, that's what. They don't know what's good for them. Cheryl, and even Mike, could never get them to come around to it."

"Come around to what?" asked John.

"That we've given them a better product than they ever imagined," said Ray.

"It *is* a pretty slick piece of software," agreed Kiki, quietly.

"They're technologically stunted over there," Ray said. "They have trouble with even the simplest things. Need us to hold their hands through everything. The problem isn't with the software, it's with them. They just don't get it."

John nodded. This was interesting, but complicated. He'd have to sort through it later. For now, he had other questions.

"Kiki, I can't find two pieces of the project that you've indicated are completed. They should be ready for Todd, but they're not."

Kiki looked at Ray. "Well, Ray must still have them, right, Ray?" she asked.

"Ray?" repeated John, dumbfounded. "Why?" *Maybe Ray was really having to doctor Kiki's work.*

"He—" started Kiki, but Ray interrupted.

"When Cheryl was here, she had me review Kiki's code before it went to testing," he said. "I've been buried, but I'll get on it."

John thought fast. *This would be a chance to see how Kiki's work looks fresh from the keyboard, before Ray has tidied things up.*

"Why don't you just send it over to me? I'll take care of it this time," said John. "That will free you up a little."

"No, you don't know the project yet," said Ray, gruffly. "I'm the only one who really does, now that Cheryl's gone."

John was surprised by his resistance. He glanced at Kiki, who had stopped fingering her spiky dark hair and was doing her best impersonation of the invisible woman, trying to be tinier than she already was.

"Don't worry, I'm a quick learner. Just shoot it over today," John said, "and I'll look at it over the long weekend."

He paused a moment, expecting an answer. Ray starred at him stonily.

I guess I'll take that as a yes, thought John. *What's his problem, anyway?*

Turning to look at Kiki, John said, "It's a long weekend, starting on Friday, and maybe the last real weekend any of us will see for a while, if we're going to meet the final deadline—and I really believe we still can—so enjoy it."

There was the sound of scraping chairs as everyone got up to leave.

"Oh, what about the speed-reading training next week?" asked Kiki, turning around. "Is it still on?"

"Speed reading?" John hated that he kept sounding like an echo. "I haven't heard anything about it." *Speed reading? Where in the world did that come from?*

"It's some corporate efficiency deal," said Todd, with a sarcastic laugh. "It's supposed to boost our productivity."

"It was scheduled a long time ago," added Kiki.

"We don't have time for that right now," said John, clearly shocked by the whole idea.

"When has that ever stopped anything from happening around here?" Todd smirked. "It's the AXD way."

John spent most of Thursday preparing for his Monday phone call with the client. It was the linchpin; he just had to find a way to make the customer see what a great product they were getting and stop all these games.

By the end of the day, he was ready to hit the road. Literally. He'd been promising his parents he would come and see their new home on the coast for weeks—well, months, actually—and with a long weekend and the promise of nothing but overtime on the horizon, he had to finally make good on that promise.

I guess I'm lucky to be getting out of the city this weekend. I really need to unwind. He signed on to his computer to look for the code he requested from Ray. It wasn't there.

Automatically, he wondered if Ray had forgotten on purpose. On the way to Ray's cube, he ran into Kiki. She looked like she was headed out for the weekend.

"Hey, boss," she said brightly, then seeing his expression, she looked worried. "Something wrong?"

"No. It's just I need to talk to Ray about something," he said.

"Uh," Kiki hesitated. "That could be a problem. He left about an hour ago."

Driving out of the city, John was still annoyed with Ray. No, with the whole situation. There was just so much working against him: an impossible-to-read customer, never-ending rewrites, a passive-aggressive employee. Add on a company that was mired in tradition and hierarchy—and speed-reading classes, believe it or not—and he'd sound just like his dad during one of his diatribes about the problems with AXD Solutions. He rolled all the windows down to clear his head.

He hit the bridge in record time. He loved this part of the drive, speeding over the water. By then, the fresh air had begun to work its magic and he'd started to entertain the thought that although this project clearly wouldn't be his brightest moment, perhaps it didn't have to be a complete disaster.

His cell rang.

"So, you're off to see the folks, huh?" said Stephanie's voice. "How are you going to handle your dad?"

Stephanie knew that his dad loved talking shop—especially during the last five years, as Tim's business career had finally begun to take off. His team was growing so rapidly, in fact, that he had actually begun hinting about John joining the airline. Not that John was totally against the idea; he just wasn't sure about his dad's radical new management ideas.

Tim might call his decision to change direction at work an epiphany; but John wondered if it wasn't more of a breakdown. *It must be what, five years now since he learned about that value-something-or-other management,* John thought. Ever since then, his dad wanted to know all about John's latest assignments—and share his concerns about AXD. John resisted these discussions. He didn't want to be rude to his father, but he also didn't want to engage him on the topic of work and hear his lecture on how he would address the problem or the concern.

"I'm not going to get into it," John said, finally. "We'll talk about his golf game."

"Good call," she said. He could tell she was a little distracted.

"Well, I gotta run," she said, lowering her voice a little. "The boss just arrived. I just wanted to wish you luck. Have a great time."

They said goodbye, and John mentally reviewed his game plan for avoiding his dad's difficult questions about his assignment: He would put the best spin on work and the new role, emphasizing what the CEO and COO had said about his "young energy" and leave it at that. He had hoped to spend a little time this weekend looking at Kiki's code, but he had brought along some of his college management textbooks instead.

He rolled the windows back up and turned up the radio. All he needed to relax was a weekend at home.

Or so he thought.

CHAPTER 2

Isn't There a Better Way?

Questioning Tradition: The First Step toward Value-Centered Management

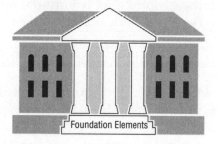

Foundation Elements

John had no trouble finding his parents' new house. He'd been to the property countless times in the decade since his parents had bought the beachfront lot. How often had he walked through the floor plan with them on paper as they'd debated

the number of gables? (They settled on three.) He remembered being astounded by all the pictures his
dad took of the foundation as it went in. *How many
pictures of a foundation does one man need?* he remembered thinking.

Still, he was surprised by the beauty and size of
the finished home. *John boy, you're not in Kansas anymore,* he teased himself as he grabbed his locker bag
from the back seat and headed for the front porch,
where he stopped, suddenly disoriented. Should he
ring the doorbell or just walk right in? He wasn't sure.
After a moment's hesitation, he compromised: He
knocked, then walked in.

"Anybody home?" he said in a loud voice.

The response was immediate. "John! You made
it!" His mother came around the corner, toweling off
her hands. He heard his father on the stairs; and he
braced himself for the inevitable question that betrayed his father's opinion of traditional management
in general: 'How are things at that mess you call a
company?'

However, the question didn't come. Instead there
were warm hugs, then he was ushered into the din-
ing room, where the table was set and dinner was
ready to be put on the table—they'd obviously been
waiting for him. He wondered guiltily how many
other weekends they'd held dinner until it was cold
when he'd called at the last minute to cancel. He was
glad he'd come.

Between passing the green beans and potatoes,
the talk centered on Stephanie, then the house, and
then the new fishing boat. Mom was painting again.
Dad had hit a hole in one for the first time. John was
happy for them, but couldn't avoid envying their relaxed lives.

"Honey, that was fabulous," his dad said at the end of the meal, pushing back his plate and winking at his wife.

She feigned annoyance. "Well, you act like you're surprised or something."

John couldn't remember how many times he'd heard the same dialogue at the end of family meals together. It made the new house seem more familiar.

"John, I was thinking we could take the boat out in the morning," his dad announced, turning away from his wife to look at him. "We just need to run down to Max's and stock up. You up to it?"

"Sure," said John, realizing how much he was looking forward to the outing.

Max's store was little more than a dilapidated shack just off the wharf. Max, the owner and only employee, was a cranky, rough-around-the-edges sort of man who would have done justice to a peg leg. When John was younger, he had often felt sorry for Max, thinking he was poor. It wasn't until just a few years ago, while in management school, that John had realized what a savvy businessman Max really was. The smell of fish, the leaning building, the sand tracked in all over the plank floor, even Max's gruff persona, were all part of the ambience that drew people to the place—and turned a profit.

They found Max in rare form. "So, you've finally come back, the prodigal son."

"Good to see you, too, Max," said John. "How's things?"

"Things? Where do you want me to start, boy?" Max was complaining about the world and seemed to be enjoying it.

Tim and John quickly grabbed as much beef jerky, cheese spread, and crackers as they could carry and headed to the counter.

"You ready?" Max asked. "Took you long enough. You're out of practice," he said, giving John a stern look. "Look, you forgot the circus peanuts," he said, throwing in a bag.

The bright orange, chewy, candy circus peanuts had been his favorite fishing snack when he was little. He couldn't recall how it had begun, but for as long as he could remember, Max had always thrown in a bag—free of charge—acting as if it were a survival necessity. These days, they never ate them, but John and his father still took the bag of candy peanuts along out of nostalgia. A few times, the candy had even come in handy as bait when the fish weren't biting anything else.

On the way out to the car, juggling their purchases, John began to wonder about his dad. Tim's silence about AXD and even his own job at the airline had made John curious. Was he waiting to lower the boom until John was a captive audience out on the water? Was something wrong? John didn't dare ask, but it made him worry.

Hours later, they were down to the circus peanuts.

They'd had a good day, eaten the junk food and even the sandwiches Linda, John's mother, had packed, talked baseball, even caught a few fish, and then they were overdue to be back at the house. John had brought along a new management book to read, but hadn't had the heart to pull it out and ignore his dad.

"You think it's about time to head back?" his dad asked, pulling his eyes away from his sketchpad.

Periodically, throughout the day, Tim had pulled out a pad of paper and appeared to be drawing something. He'd never been the artistic type, so John was curious, but had held his tongue.

"Yeah, in a minute. First, you gonna tell me what you're doing with the pad?" John asked.

Tim raised his eyebrows and announced, "Just drawing the structure."

"Yeah, I know. You and mom did a great job. The house is beautiful," said John, looking at his parents' place, far away on the distant shore.

His dad looked up, confused, then followed John's eyes to the house. "Oh," he said. "Not the house. This is something different. It's something I've been thinking about for a long time."

John looked over at the drawing resting on his dad's knee. It appeared to be a crude drawing of the new house: one large rectangle, topped by three vertical pillars supporting a triangular roof.

"What is it, then?" John asked.

His dad paused for a moment. "You know," he said, suddenly hesitant. "It's Value-Centered Management. A while ago I found a way to diagram it, to put the whole idea down on paper. I was just fiddling with it a little." He paused. "Oh, you don't want to hear about this anyway. It's nothing." Tim began to put away the notebook.

The words made John uneasy, partly because he was worried about getting trapped in a long discussion, but also because his dad had obviously sensed John's unwillingness to talk business and was making an effort to restrain his enthusiasm for the topic.

What would it hurt to hear him out? John wondered. He braced himself and said. "Actually, I'd like to see it."

His dad stopped trying to stuff the pad into his bag. He looked skeptical. "You sure? You're not obligated."

John just nodded his willingness.

"You know, I've been in corporate America for more than two decades now," Tim said, thoughtfully, looking out over the bay. "And most businesses set their direction and tactical plans based on traditional business education. I see you brought along one of your textbooks," Tim said, nodding toward the waterproof bag on the deck. "But there are a lot of gaps in the things we've done traditionally, so I always felt I was running into roadblocks."

Most businesses set their direction and tactical plans based on traditional business education.

John was surprised at how closely his dad was describing his own feelings.

Tim continued: "It was frustrating because most business solutions require people to work together, but in the way most businesses are set up, the different knowledge sources are segregated from each other, in departments. Well, that motivates people to build their own kingdoms. And then you're stuck with people trying to jockey for position and prove their worth instead of actually getting results for customers. I kept asking myself, 'If we're all focusing on our own interests, then who is focused on the customer?' The answer was nobody."

In a quieter voice, Tim admitted. "And then, one day, I finally got fed up and asked myself, 'Who says the way we've always done things is the best way to do them? 'Who said so?'"

As the boat slowly rocked, Tim looked over at John, as if trying to gauge his reaction, then went on.

"Not long after that, I bumped into a different approach to management. I've been diagramming it here."

He held it out to John; and John took it. Now he could see the complete house diagram where the bottom rectangle read simply, *Foundation Elements,* and the first pillar was labeled *Value* in his dad's trademark slanted handwriting:

Just then, John's attention was distracted by the sound of a motor drawing nearer. A bright red boat was heading straight toward them.

"Ahoy, you landlubbers!" the booming voice carried across the water.

"Hey, it's Vic, Vic Carr. You remember him, right?" Tim asked. John did, vaguely. He had a much clearer memory of Vic's daughter, Beth, however. He'd had a crush on her for years, and was disappointed to hear a few years back that she'd married a fancy business guy from the city.

As the boat passed closer, Vic cut the motor and called out to them, "Ahoy, lads. Wanted to let you know we're having a little shindig tomorrow night at our place. Why don't you come over; all of you," he said, nodding in John's direction. "It's been a while."

"I'll have to check with the boss," answered Tim, "but I think we can make it."

"About seven, then. It's just a casual thing. See you there," he said, firing up the engine and speeding off toward shore with a wave.

For a moment, caught in his wake, the two of them stood in the swaying boat watching the craft grow smaller. Then, John remembered the drawing in his dad's hand and made a decision. What did he have to lose? He took a deep breath.

"You know, Dad, I'm not quite ready to call it a day yet. He motioned to the drawing. Why don't you drop anchor, break out some of those horrible peanuts and tell me some more."

An hour later, John's head was spinning as he tied up the boat and walked the short distance to the house. *The whole thing—what did his dad call it? Value-Centered Management? It's like an iceberg,* he thought. *It might look like very little on the surface, but it's really miles deep.*

He reviewed the conversation on the water as he climbed into a cool shower and then into a comfortable recliner in his room.

His dad had told him, "The focus of Value-Centered Management is finding out and providing what the customer values. The end customer keeps everyone in business, so there's really no higher form of management than managing a customer's value and his desire to give you money. That's what actually pays the bills, what pays your salary. Our job is to find what the customer values, center our organization around it, and then continue to find it until the whole organization is working together to get it done."

At that point, Tim had looked at John's face and must have read the disappointment written there.

"That's it?" John had asked, skeptically.

"It sounds simple, but it isn't," Tim warned. "Value-Centered Management is an aggressive approach to streamlining an organization completely around what the customer values. You have to dig down deep past what your customers are *saying* they want and figure out what they *really* value and will pay anything to get. Then you have to have the courage to look at your business again from their perspective. And then you've got to change, really change."

"It doesn't sound like rocket science, Dad," said John skeptically. "I think we do that every time we meet with a customer to draw up specs."

"Then why isn't your customer satisfied when you meet those specs or thrilled when you exceed them?" Tim asked pointedly.

John froze in disbelief. "Mentec? How could you know about—" He couldn't have been more shocked if he had suddenly been plunged into the chilly water lapping the side of the boat.

His father raised his hand to stop him. "I didn't know anything about Mentec, specifically, but I can guess what's happening. I spent years wondering how my customers could be so unhappy with me when I was doing everything I could think of to make them happy."

His father had begun to speak more rapidly then, reflecting the energy behind his words. He explained how more successful business people focused on building cultures that support the pursuit of customer value. "Then, they're reviewing how they structure teams within their organizations to work collaboratively so that everything needed to serve a customer in the best way is available and set up in a way to allow value to flow seamlessly."

"Hey, look at your line, a fish bit the peanut!" his dad had shouted, dropping the drawing momentarily into the water in his excitement. John had then reeled in the biggest fish of the day. Secretly, he wondered if his dad hadn't brought home an even bigger catch. The things his dad was saying made sense to John. He was going for them, hook, line, and sinker.

Alone now, with more time to think, John wondered: *Could our first problem with Mentec really be as basic as not having a clear understanding of what they value?* Certainly, that would explain the constant rewrites and the innuendo surrounding the project.

"The customer is completely unreasonable," Mike had claimed in the managers' meeting. "They say what we're creating isn't what they pictured and described."

Ray's angry face flashed into John's mind. "These people are never happy," he had said. "We've given them a better product than they ever dreamed."

It seems more like a nightmare to me, John thought foggily. From outside his window, he heard the low whoosh of the ocean on the breakers. He pictured the waves lapping and crashing, flowing toward some unknown destination. It was the last thing he remembered thinking when he woke up the next morning.

The first thing John noticed when he opened his eyes was *pink*. The spare bedroom was pink. He'd have to talk to his mom about that, he decided. He caught a whiff of breakfast cooking, which motivated him to get out of the armchair, or he might have been tempted to go back to sleep for a few more hours. *But man cannot live on junk food alone,* he sighed, rubbing his gnawing stomach.

Today, the plan was to go into town, he thought happily as he showered. (He kept smelling fish. Was it his hands?) Entering the kitchen, a few minutes later, he kissed his mom on the cheek as she stood at the stove, scrambling eggs.

"The dead arise," she said, teasingly. "Last night, we tried to wake you up in the chair, but you were out for the count. You okay?" she asked, turning around to give him a good looking over.

"Fine," he said. "Great. I think I just got too much sun. I've been spending a lot of time in the office lately. Oh, and, Mom, why is my room pink?"

"Pink? That's not pink, that's coral. Coral and chocolate brown. It's very current. I'm surprised you don't know that," she sniffed.

Tim joined them just as they sat down at the table. He looked eager to get going into town, too, and wolfed down his food almost as quickly as John did.

It took less than five minutes to drive to the little downtown district. They parked on a side street and began to stroll slowly down the block, ducking into any store they chose. At eleven o'clock, they found themselves midway between two competing coffee shops. They were extraordinarily similar. Each served the town's trademark Seaside Roast, with only slight variations. Both took orders through a window, as their customers stood on the sidewalk outside.

"Have you given any thought to our conversation yesterday?" Tim asked him, sitting down on a wooden bench surrounded by pigeons. The birds looked up expectantly, anticipating a potential sprinkling of biscotti crumbs.

John sat down beside him.

"Actually, I can't get it out of my mind," John said. He was startled by a flutter as the disappointed pigeons took off in search of better prospects.

Tim laughed. "That's how I was when I started down this path," he said. "Value-Centered Management requires you to accept that you don't know everything you probably should about your customer. You've got to ask a lot of questions."

Value-Centered Management requires you to accept that you don't know everything you probably should about your customer.

"But where do you start? It feels a little overwhelming," admitted John.

"You begin by asking fundamental questions. For example, look at these two coffee shops. What causes a person to want to do business with one of them over the other? I think it'll help us understand what makes a person want to spend their money with AXD over a competing business."

John looked closely at the storefronts of the two coffee houses. Which would he choose? Probably the one with the richest smell and the best-looking blend; he went for quality. But he knew his mom would be looking for cleanliness and a smiling server; his dad for extras like a great pastry or two on display. As he studied the stores, he noticed two surfers, with wet sand still coating their shorts and legs, carefully counting their quarters and looking closely at the menus. They'd choose the least expensive, he guessed.

"That's not easy," said John. "There are so many customers with so many competing interests."

"Right, and then, within your company, there are even more where that came from. Just ask yourself, what does your sales department value? Well, they want to boost sales, because they get rewarded for that. What does IT value? They want to complete all the internal work tickets. They get rewarded for that. Different departments within the same company have very different values.

"And that leads to the staggering question: How many competing values should there be in an organization? The answer, of course, is one: What the customer values."

John was silent, contemplating the magnitude of what his father was saying.

"But to do that, you'd have to change everything," John finally blurted out.

"Exactly. And most businesses—and their leaders—aren't willing to ask the big questions like these for that very reason. It comes down to this: Do you have the courage to seek out what your customer truly values, and then do something about it?"

It wasn't the type of question that required an answer; that was good, because John wasn't sure what to say.

The time passed quickly, and they got back to the house with just enough time to get dressed before heading to the Carrs' house.

Their house was easy to find. The yard was lit with colorful lanterns that flickered a kaleidoscope of color. Laughter spilled out from the house and deck. As they drew closer, they could hear soft jazz playing in the background.

It was a perfect night, John thought, as he finished up several introductions and wandered out onto the deck. He pulled a note from his pocket. His father had given it to him as they left for the party. It was a drawing of just the rectangular foundation, labeled *Foundation Elements*. Five new notations had been added in a bold hand:

Foundation Elements

Visual workplace

Time management

Cost reduction

Reduction of nonvalue-added activities

Resources reallocation

Food for thought: The foundation of any business has to be sound, or nothing you build on it will last.

There was a hastily scribbled Post-it note stuck on the bottom, which looked as though his dad was racing to keep up with his thoughts. "Food for thought: The foundation of any business has to be sound, or nothing you build on it will last."

"Is it a love letter? Who's it from?" the laughing voice was laced with a rich Spanish accent. Instinctively, John folded the paper up and put it in his pocket. "Oh, it *is* a love letter! I knew it!" John didn't recognize the trilling laugh.

He turned to find Mrs. Carr standing beside him. She didn't wait for him to collect his thoughts.

"Your father tells me you're doing some work for Mentec," she said. "It's a small world. My son-in-law, Frank, works at Mentec. He and Beth are living in the city now, did you know?"

"Frank? Frank Bowen?" asked John with a stutter.

Mrs. Carr nodded, but then someone called her name and she smiled an apologetic goodbye. "Excuse me," she murmured and turned to meet an arriving guest. John felt a little dizzy.

It couldn't be, he told himself. It would be too incredible a coincidence. However, the funny thing was, the man he was scheduled to call first thing Monday morning, the unreasonable client, the man no one could please, was also named Frank. Frank Bowen.

The party ended late, and John slept in until almost lunch the next day. He was awakened by a forceful knock on his door. *Definitely not mom,* he thought wryly.

"Hey, I'm hiking down to the sandwich shop in about thirty minutes. You want to tag along?" his dad shouted the question through the door.

John hesitated. He did and he didn't. He had questions but was a little afraid of the answers.

"Hey, can you hear me in there? Are you awake?" More loud pounding.

"Sorry!" John roused himself. "I'll be ready in ten. Meet you downstairs."

It took him close to a half-hour to shower and pull on some clothes, but his dad didn't mention it. In fact, his dad was in a good-humored mood as they walked through a trail in the woods down to the shop.

"I had an agenda in inviting you here," Tim said as they entered the café, the bell on the door jingling brightly. "I'll order, you watch them make the sandwiches," he said.

By the time they had moved to the front of the line, John had observed as the workers made six different sandwiches, hot and cold, out of four types of bread, all without moving more than a step or two from their original positions. He'd never noticed before how organized—no, *orchestrated and focused*—the process could be.

"Lean over the counter for a second. Do you notice the signs in front of each workstation?" his father asked. "They're there so everyone knows what to do and how to do it."

"This is a great example of the first foundational element of a Value-Centered Culture: a visual workplace," his dad said. "They've got the process spelled out and posted where everyone can see it so everyone knows what to do, how to do it, when to do it, and where to do it."

"The best visual workplaces follow something we call SAFE-T," his dad said, writing it out on a napkin. "I forgot to bring a notepad, so this will have to do. SAFE-T stands for five steps to workplace order and efficiency. When I go into a workplace—any workplace—I automatically look to see if they're doing five things: Separate what is not needed; Arrange in order the things that *are* needed; Finish with inspection for potential abnormalities; then use standardization tools to ensure that everyone understands the rules. Are you still with me?" Tim asked, looking up at John. Seeing that John was, he continued. "Finally, an efficient business has to Test constantly to confirm the system is working."

John studied the napkin for a moment:

Separate what is not needed.

Arrange in order.

Finish with inspection.

Everyone should understand the rules.

Test constantly to confirm the system is working.

Tim added, "You can see most of that happening here with the sandwich makers. Notice that there's nothing lying around that isn't absolutely needed. No extra knives, just one for the team member who slices the bread. They've separated out what isn't necessary to the process."

John studied the preparation area with new eyes. The bread and sandwich toppings were arranged in perfect order. "They've got everything they need within arm's reach," he said out loud.

"And not too much or too little of any ingredient is out at once. Just enough for the next batch of sandwiches," his dad added. "And they've got the most failproof inspection system around," he said. "The customer stands there and watches the product being built, correcting any errors along the way."

John had to admit he was impressed.

"Okay, but this is more like a manufacturing facility, in a way. They're building a physical product. Can it work in a pure service environment like ours?" asked John.

"That's the beauty of it," said Tim. "The process can work anywhere, with anything."

"That is," he added. "If you've got nerve enough to break from the traditional way of doing things. Not everyone does."

They had filled 15 napkins with notes on creating a visual workplace and were moving into the second foundation element of Value-Centered Management—time management—when the alarm on Tim's watch went off, reminding him of a conference call in twenty minutes.

"Nonvalue-added time is the big issue in time management," Tim said as they got up from the booth, stretching their cramped limbs. "That is the time when nothing productive is happening, no value is being added. Either you're stuck waiting for the next step, or you are doing things within a process that aren't adding value to the customer. You want to reduce nonvalue-added time and maximize value-added time because that's when things are being done that your customer is willing to pay for."

During the walk home, Tim explained how to calculate customer pace time, which he defined as what a company needs to produce on a standard frequency to satisfy the customer, whether hourly, daily, weekly, or monthly. John remembered hearing about something similar in college but had never used it, considering it a tool more fitted to the manufacturing industry. Now, he could see how it just might help his team to work out a schedule for meeting the final deadline of their services.

"Lean principles work everywhere," Tim said as they entered the house. He headed up the stairs to his home office, taking them two at a time. "Remember that, and you're miles ahead of everyone else. We'll have to talk later." John was surprised to find that he was anticipating the chance to continue the discussion.

John spent the next hour with his mom on the front porch, facing the water, getting the update on what the crazy extended family was up to. Eventually, his mother's face grew serious, as she said in a low voice, "You'll never know how much it means to your dad to talk about business with you the way you are now. He's been wanting to speak to you about it for years. He wants so much for you to avoid the same frustrations he went through. You were young, you didn't see it all, but the early years at the airline were hard on him."

John felt a lump in his throat and didn't dare speak.

They continued to sit in silence, listening to the rhythmic crashing of the waves below and the call of an occasional seagull until his dad joined them.

"You know what would be ideal?" Tim asked, sitting down with them.

John couldn't think of anything better than the current moment and he shook his head.

"The ideal situation is someone paying you for something it didn't take you anything to produce."

"Tim!" Linda swatted his arm in protest. "Here we are, having a nice time, and all you can think of is

business! I'm going in," she said and moved toward
the door. "Then you can talk business all you want in
peace." Linda cast Tim an angry look, but winked at
John as she passed.

When the screen door had slammed shut behind
her, John said, "Well, you sure know how to clear a
room."

Tim looked sheepish. "She complains, but she
doesn't really mind," he said. "I was just saying that
smart leaders focus on developing multiple revenue
streams while removing barriers to profit; the ideal situation is someone paying you for something that
didn't cost you anything extra to produce."

"That seems pretty simple," said John, who had
been drifting off to sleep before his father arrived. He
stood to stretch.

"That's right. It's so simple that most leaders miss
it," Tim replied.

Tim was hooked. He mined his father's knowledge
base for more information as the clock ticked closer to
the time he had to head back to the city for his morning call with Mentec.

"Efficiency efforts have proven that an amazing 70
to 95 percent of the work within a company adds no
value. You've seen for yourself how time is wasted in
organizations in an effort to stay true to procedures
and policies simply because they are procedures and
policies and not because they are necessarily right to
create value for the organization," Tim said, just as
the grandfather clock in the hall struck six. It was
time for John to go.

"One last thing," his father, raised a finger. "Look
to see if you can identify any of these nonvalue-added
activities in your area. You'll know them when you see
them." He quickly scribbled down what seemed to be a
long list:

Seven Nonvalue-added Activities

- **Overproviding:** Providing more product, work, time and/or servicing than necessary to serve your customers.

- **Unnecessary waiting:** Any time customers or team members are waiting for something or someone when there is no value being added.

- **Unnecessary quantities:** Having a higher quantity of items or information than necessary to do the job required in the operation.

- **Unnecessary movement:** The unnecessary movement of items, people, or a person within an operation or process.

- **Repeat work:** Having to do something over again because it was not done right the first time.

- **Irrelevant work:** Doing things within an operation that are irrelevant to the customer.

- **Underutilized resources:** People or machines that are not being fully used to their potential to provide value to the client.

John scanned the paper.

Some of the terms were familiar, others weren't.

"Well, I can see one right off the top of my head," said John. "All the rewrites we're doing. It's repeat work. We're doing it over again because we didn't get it right the first time."

"Right, and the second time, you're doing it at your own expense. There's no value added, because Mentec isn't paying you for the time it takes to fix your mistakes."

Tim rubbed his temples and said, "Well, I've given you most of what you need to start building a Value-Centered Enterprise; it's all wrapped up in the fundamentals we've gone over this weekend: visual workplace, time management, cost reduction, and reduction of nonvalue-added resources. We'll talk about resource reallocation later."

John let out a breath of air and pushed back from the table. "I've got a long drive, and you need to get back to your normal life," he said. "I shouldn't have kept you talking like this all weekend, but it just makes so much sense . . . once I decided to listen."

John paused. "I really owe you one, dad," he said sincerely.

"Actually, you'll owe me a million by the time we're done," replied Tim. "But who's counting?"

John drove with the windows down. He didn't feel tired but wanted to be alert and safe. He was lucky, and reached the ferry just in time for its last crossing. Just one other vehicle boarded with him. He got out of the car and stood at the rail, feeling mentally exhilarated. For the first time in a long time, he had a plan, a direction, and a focus. His cell rang.

"Hey, John," his father said. "On Monday morning, do me a favor. Don't call Mentec. Go to see them. And plan to stay there afterward for a while. Just . . . just plan to stay all day."

John was confused. "Why? I—"

"You can't do anything until you go see for yourself what's going on over there at Mentec, and you can't do that on the phone. You'll laugh, but we call it the Go-Gos. Go see, go hear, go touch, go smell, and go taste if necessary. Don't accept anyone else's word, but spend the day observing Mentec's processes and asking questions. Soak it all up like a sponge."

"I guess I can do that," said John.

"You know what sponges do, don't you?" asked his dad, persistently.

"What?"

"Well, for one thing, they don't talk a lot. They listen," said Tim. "Tomorrow, just listen."

Just then, John must have hit a dead spot, because the call ended abruptly. Or maybe in his enthusiasm, his dad had simply hung up; he sometimes did that. John didn't mind. Over the last few days, his dad had given him the key to beginning to build a new and stronger relationship with Mentec, resting on the Foundation Elements of Value-Centered Management. It was a very strong beginning. And he wouldn't have to go it alone.

CHAPTER 3

How Can I Be Sure to Deliver What My Customers Value?

Value: *The Difference between What They Say They Want and What They Will Pay Anything to Get*

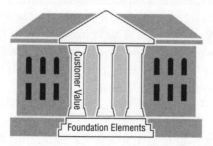

John wasn't sure if it was the four cups of coffee or the energy from his father's new ideas but, whatever the reason, he felt better than he had in months as he pulled into the parking lot at AXD Software.

It was early but, already, the smell of hot tar hung in the air, and with no clouds in sight, the morning sun hitting his dirty windshield was blinding. *It's going to be a scorcher,* he thought, as he cracked his car windows. He strode quickly to the building, his mind racing. He had to call Frank Bowen and request that their morning meeting be in person, instead of over the telephone, then fill Mike from sales in on the change of plans because he had been planning to join in the call.

Luckily, he ran into Mike at the elevators.

"Speak of the devil," said Mike, "I was just telling Dan here that I hoped you had a good breakfast today, it being your last meal and all."

John grinned. "Don't forget, you're in this with me, right up to your skinny neck.

By the way," John said, "I was just going to track you down. About our meeting today with Mentec, I'm changing the call to an in-person meeting, so that I can get a better read on what's happening over there."

"Can't say that's a bad idea, but, unfortunately, I can't make it." The smile on Mike's face betrayed the relief he felt. "I'm scheduled for another conference call right after Mentec. You'll have to go it alone."

As he watched Mike walk away through the closing elevator doors, John felt his confident morning buzz deflating like a balloon.

John's Plan B fizzled, too. After Mike ditched him, his plan was to take Ray, his senior programmer, but he wasn't at his desk yet. Plan C materialized when Blake arrived, carrying a new tropical plant for his cube. John gave the plant a month, tops, to survive in the harsh fluorescent lighting. Blake seemed absolutely overjoyed by the invitation to the client meeting.

"Well, it's official, Kiki's code is ready for graphics!" he told John, as he set down the plant on his desk.

"What code? The code Todd said he didn't have on Thursday?" John asked, dumbfounded. "I thought I asked Ray to send it to me."

"Well, I don't know. Todd said he got it Thursday night, just before we all took off." He looked at John's face and said, hesitantly. "Sorry, I thought you knew."

John wasn't sure how to react. The words of his Little League coach echoed in his head like a mantra. *Shake it off. Shake it off.* Funny, he even felt a little like he'd been hit in the chest with a fastball.

"No, that's great. It's good that we're moving that code forward again," he said, letting out a deep breath of air. After a moment's silence, he asked. "How does it look?"

"I haven't seen it, but Todd says it's as slick as usual," said Blake. "I wish I knew what the problem with Mentec is, though."

"That, my friend, is the million-dollar question," said John.

Mentec's building leaned out over the street, all glass and structural steel. It was designed to look like it was tipping, something that John remembered got a lot of press when it was under construction.

Frank's office was on the eighth floor. He wasn't in when they arrived, but his assistant seated them and offered them coffee.

The office was big, but not pretentious. It had a clean, unpersonalized look, which felt stripped down to the basics. There was, however, one framed picture on the desk, facing away from John. He was sure it was of Frank and Beth, and he was about to get up and steal a peek, when the door opened and Frank walked in.

He wasn't what John had imagined. Not quite as starched or trendy as his position might have suggested. And, most surprisingly, he didn't seem to be angry, either.

John and Blake stood to greet him. John didn't mention Beth, thinking it wasn't the time.

"Why don't we sit over there," Frank said, motioning to a small conference table. "Some members of my group are joining us. Honestly, we're glad to see you. Jay Jackson has nothing but good to say about you."

"Jay Jackson from Trenneth?" asked John, feeling slightly disoriented. He remembered bumping into Mr. Jackson in the Thai restaurant just the other day.

"Right. Trenneth is our warehousing subsidiary. Didn't you know? This software that's been giving us so many headaches interfaces with the program you created for him last year. The warehousing one. We've got high hopes now that you're on the job that we'll be able to—oh, great, here they are."

A man and a woman strode into the room, their faces hard and set. Instinctively, John braced himself. *This is the attitude I anticipated,* he thought.

"John and Blake, this is Tracy and Ramon. They're heading up this project."

The two barely glanced at John. Obviously, their hopes for his ability to turn things around did not equal Frank's.

"Well," said Frank, "we'll turn the time over to you, John. Where do you want to start?"

"With a tour," said John. Out of the corner of his eye, he saw Tracy and Ramon look up at him, curiously. Obviously, this was not what they had expected.

"I need you to show me how and where the software will be used," continued John, a little heartened that he'd disoriented them. "And I need to talk to the people who will be using it. I'm thinking it will take a few hours. How are your schedules?"

"We can make it work. Anything to get us back on track," said Frank. "Tracy and Ramon will take it from here. Why don't we all get together for lunch at Bisquotti's afterward? It's on me. I'll be eager to hear your take on where we go next."

"So will I," added John, under his breath. *Dad, you got me into this. I really hope you know what you're doing.*

Their first stop was the phone bank. The sound of humming voices was a relief after the overwhelming silence of the past few minutes on the elevator.

John watched as a woman sitting near him with a pencil stuck behind one ear and a headset on the other typed something out slowly on a keyboard, using only her index finger.

"A new hire?" he asked, motioning in her direction.

"That's Margaret," said Tracy. "Been here five years. Believe it or not, she's our top inbound producer. Over one million dollars in sales last year."

John was floored, and not for the last time. Mentec was full of surprises. For one thing, the computer hardware was more than five years old, and their office suite was three releases behind. *Could they even run the software we're creating on these ancient machines?* John wondered.

It wasn't just the hardware that was behind the times. In an impromptu focus group meeting, where they gathered a few employees to try out the software and offer feedback, he noticed several individuals struggling with the interface.

Toward the end of the focus group, one employee vented her frustration: "Ugh!" she said, growling at the computer screen. "Why can't we just keep doing things the way we've always done them? It's worked okay up to now." Around the table, every single head nodded in agreement, reminding John of the row of bobble heads his grandmother used to have on her car dashboard. As a kid, he used to laugh at them, but not right now.

After most of the employees had filed out of the room, Ramon explained, "The software you guys are creating makes the delivery process paperless. That's great for our bottom line, but hard on our people. Our team members are used to getting an order, printing it out, and cycling the hard copy through the delivery process. This changes everything for them."

Blake, who was shutting down the laptop, observed casually. "Well, it's obvious we need to simplify the system, if it's going to work for them. We need to cut the functionality back to the bare minimum, for now."

Hearing him, Tracy and Ramon almost jumped out of their seats. "That's exactly what we've been saying!" Ramon slapped the table in triumph. "Exactly what we've been saying all along. We need something simple that does the job, but doesn't overwhelm everyone who is used to doing it the old way."

Their outburst stunned Blake, who had just been thinking out loud. But now a slow smile of realization crossed his face, as he looked into John's incredulous eyes. For the first time, Tracy smiled. Ramon rocked back in his chair with his hands over his eyes, and let out a long, loud breath of air, then sat back up, shaking his head, "You guys just don't know how frustrating this has been."

The room fell silent, but the mood was comfortable for the first time. "Gentlemen, I think it's time for lunch," said Tracy, finally. "I think we've got something to celebrate."

Two hours later, Blake and John were on their way back to the office. Over lunch, they had laid out a plan for Frank that involved simplifying the software to ensure it was compatible with Mentec's hardware and workforce needs. Frank was in.

John couldn't believe his luck, and luck was the only way he could explain what had just happened. He had walked in with no clear idea of how he would save this contract, and it had all fallen into place like clockwork. He couldn't have planned it better.

Back at the office, he called a quick team meeting to update his group. As he watched them enter the conference room, he could tell that Blake had already filled them in on some of what had happened. Kiki was smiling, though quiet. Blake was grinning ear to ear, commenting and laughing loudly. Ray looked angry. He came in last, leaving a few empty chairs between himself and the rest of the group. However, Todd's reaction was the most unexpected. He watched the group with a bemused expression on his face and did not join in. Although he sat near them, his casual disdain made him seem even more separate from the group than Ray.

"Blake and I just got back from a meeting with Mentec. It went better than we could have dared to hope," said John, smiling. "Tomorrow morning, we'll have a longer meeting here at nine o'clock to make assignments. Right now, I just want to give you an update."

John glanced at Blake and noticed how hard he was trying not to interrupt and tell the story himself. It looked physically painful. "Blake, why don't you go over the changes we're going to make to the software," John offered.

Glancing at Ray, who was holding perfectly still, John added, "But first, I want to say that this team has created a fine piece of software, one we can be proud of. Our client has simply requested a slightly different direction."

As Blake spoke about the process of simplification, John watched Ray. Although he held perfectly still, the air around him seemed to pulse with rage. John kept waiting—almost hoping—for an outburst, but it never came. When the meeting ended, Ray simply stood and walked out of the room without a word.

That night, John called his dad. Tim answered the phone on the first ring without a greeting.

"How'd it go?" his gruff voice boomed through the phone. Usually his dad's abruptness bothered John, but this time it made him smile. He could sense the concern behind the bravado. *Had it always been there?* he wondered.

He didn't keep his dad in suspense long. John quickly explained the meeting, the tour, the impromptu focus group—and the moment when it all came together.

"I don't know, it was just magic, that's the only way I can explain it," said John. "Everything just fell into place."

"That's not *magic*," his dad's tone was jubilant. "That's Value-Centered Management. It's what I've been telling you about. When you actually find out what a customer values—that's when good things start to happen.

"Right now you are meeting a nonvalue-added demand, just like you should," said Tim.

"Whoa, why are you calling it nonvalue-added?" asked John, concerned. "Mentec hated us; now they love us. Isn't that adding value?"

"Well, yes and no," said Tim. "Yes, because you are doing exactly what you need to do right now. You are succeeding in correcting a past failure, deficiency, or error. It's a demand you have to meet because AXD didn't get the software right the first time. But it doesn't add anything new to your bottom line."

Tim paused as if waiting for a response from John. When it didn't come, he continued.

"Son, what you're doing with Mentec right now is critical, All I'm saying is that you're not making any money on it," he said, finally. "But you already know that. Once you get these problems corrected and are going forward, you're going to be looking to provide value-added demand. That means you're going to be looking to meet a demand that your customer is willing to pay additional money for. But we'll talk more about that later.

"Right now, you've got to think about how to keep those good things happening. Do you have a plan?" asked Tim.

John didn't answer immediately. His dad's response wasn't what he had expected; and, to be honest, he had hoped he was done with fact-finding.

"Well, tomorrow, we're having a meeting with my team to make assignments," he began, "and—"

"Sure, well, that's important," said Tim. "But that's not what I'm asking. You know what your customer wants *today,* at this moment. But what about two weeks from now? What will be the thing they want most *then*? What are you going to do to keep current with what your customer values? To keep the magic flowing?"

What are you going to do to keep current with what your customer values?

John was stumped. Did his dad really want him to do this whole thing every two weeks?

"Tell me about this Blaine or Blake guy you took with you," Tim said. "You mentioned he was the one who first identified the value point for Mentec. Could he be the bridge between your client and you? Every

Value-Centered Enterprise has to have a Value Management Service Team—or in smaller groups like yours—a person, who stays on top of customer needs and taps the resources to meet them. You said this guy of yours got along with your clients and was excited by what happened at Mentec. Sounds like he's got enthusiasm, too.

"Well, if he's the guy, he's going to need to put together a team of customers at Mentec that can be his Customer Value Committee. They're the ones who work with him to identify what their company values."

John could hear his father's voice continuing on in the background, but he wasn't tracking with him. He was a little put off by his dad's suggestion. *I mean, it was one thing to be right about getting to know what my client values, but if he's suggesting that I reorganize my department, well, that's going a little bit too far.* He'd never even heard of a Value Management whatchamacallit before, anyway.

"John, John, are you with me?" his dad's voice blared through the phone.

"Look, Dad, we already have a bridge; sales is the interface between us and the customer," said John, buying himself some time to think. "And Blake is a programmer. That's his job . . . a full-time job."

John was acutely aware of the awkward silence on the other end of the phone, even the construction sounds had stopped, but he didn't know what to do with it. After a moment, his dad began again, in a gentler voice.

"Remember when we first started thinking about building the new house?" Tim asked. "The old place had so many memories. There were so many arguments for staying. We were surrounded by our friends there, and we were comfortable," he said. "It was a good place."

"Sure," said John, deciding to play along.

"But it could never be some of the things we wanted. It could never be on the beach, where I could fish. It could never be larger or have more light, like your mom wanted. We had to make a choice: Stay in our comfort zone, without some of the things we wanted, or take a leap of faith and change," he said.

"Coming here was the best move we ever made," he said. "You know where I am right now?" he asked. Tim didn't wait for an answer. "I'm sitting out here on the dock, watching the stars come out. Son, it just doesn't get any better than this."

John said goodbye and set down the phone. The magnitude of what his dad was suggesting was beginning to sink in. It wasn't just a one-time deviation from the traditional way of doing things; he wanted John to completely change the way he did business. John wasn't sure he was ready for that.

He was sure of one thing, however: He didn't want to think about it anymore tonight. He flipped on the television and found a *M*A*S*H* rerun. He dreamed that night that he was a military surgeon, operating on Mentec's computer program. The faster he typed, the louder the other doctors in the room shouted that it had never been done that way, that it wouldn't work. Ray was among them, his two angry eyes all that showed above a green surgical mask. Somehow, John knew that what he was doing was the cure, the solution. In one more moment, he would know if he had succeeded in saving the software.

And then, suddenly, he was awake, feeling cold and cramped from his night on the sofa, and angry that he had awakened before he knew how things turned out in his dream. He stood up and cracked the blinds to peer out into the street. The sun was just coming up.

He limped into the shower to wake up, turning the shower head to the strongest pulse to loosen his tightened neck muscles. As he began to feel human again, he realized that, somehow, during the night, he'd reached a conclusion. He was going to follow his dad's advice. It was the best option he had at this point.

Getting out of the shower, he got dressed and called his dad. Tim was already awake, and together they put together a challenging schedule that would allow John's team to meet their drop-dead date for Mentec.

"Most people think of Customer Pace Time as a manufacturing concept, only," said Tim. "It's ignored, for the most part, in the service industry. But it can work anywhere. The concept is simple: Take what you need to produce to satisfy the customer. In your case, this is the number of modules that you must complete or revise. Divide it by the actual time allotted for actual work to be done. How many days do you have to get this done on time? The result is the pace at which the operation must move to ensure it meets the demands of its customers."

Together, he and his father were careful to schedule in time for Blake to meet with the customer each week to define the changes to be made to existing modules. For new modules, Blake would create complete specs. As a result, Blake's programming time would be cut dramatically, requiring Kiki and Ray to shoulder more responsibility.

"Your Value Management Service Team Member and the Customer Value Committee are critical," his dad said as they finished off the new Gantt chart.

"Once Blake pulls that team together, it'll save you money. Too many businesses waste capital on sales and marketing, guessing at what their customers want. It's more effective to get together with your customers regularly and *ask* them specifically what they want."

"So, sales and marketing aren't necessary?" asked John, cradling the phone with his shoulder as he buttered a piece of toast.

"Oh, no, they've got their role," replied Tim. "It's just that the relationship with your customer has to be organized and maintained all year. And the Value Management Service Team Member must be able to translate what your customers are saying into specifics that your team can understand and fulfill. It just requires a different skill set than maybe sales and marketing have. They catch the fish, but it's your job to prepare and cook it the way the customer wants it.

"Hey, while I've got you on the phone, do you still have that drawing of the house with three pillars?" Tim asked. John pulled a tattered and water-stained paper from his wallet. "Finding value is the first pillar," said Tim. John stared down at his dad's slanted letters, spelling out *Value.*

"That's where we are now. But we can't just forget about the Foundation Elements. Imagine that you are lowering a dam to let the water out. The dam represents your costs and the water is revenue held behind. Value Centered Management is an aggressive approach to streamlining an organization completely around the customer's desire, and reviewing how we structure our group so that the complete organization is working collaboratively and cost-effectively to achieve that purpose. You've got an idea of what the customer values, now you have to rethink how your organization can deliver it."

"Well, besides changing Blake's role, I can think of one thing right off the top. That insane speed-reading course my people are supposed to go to next week," said John. "I don't see how it will really benefit Mentec."

"Could be that's irrelevant work and needs to go," said Tim.

"And I have a hunch about the work flow between Kiki and Ray. There's a backlog there, and I'm not sure what Kiki really is capable of doing. She's been kind of hidden in Ray's shadow for so long."

"She could be underutilized. Good. You've got the right idea. And here's a great place to start: Today, go into the office and focus on the visual workplace. Remember, that's the thing we talked about at the sandwich shop. Examine your people's workspaces and go through the five SAFE-T steps." John glanced down at the scribbled list:

Separate what is not needed.

Arrange in order.

Finish with inspection.

Everyone should understand the rules.

Test constantly to confirm the system is working.

Looking at it, John was a little disappointed. "But why waste time with that when—"

"Trust me, this won't be a waste of time," said Tim, firmly. "That's the mistake too many managers make, thinking the physical environment doesn't contribute to productivity problems. You're sending Blake back to Mentec today to get the exact idea of what to do with the first few modules. He's moving the work on value forward. You can focus on the productivity issues in your office. Do it. You'll see."

John agreed. He hung up and headed to the bedroom to finish getting dressed. Digging in his sock drawer, he came across his lucky socks, black with his college insignia on the ankles. He hadn't worn them for years, but, after a moment, he pulled them on. He figured with what he had decided to do today, he'd need all the luck he could get.

The staff meeting was a repeat of the day before: Blake exuberant, Kiki quietly cooperative and supportive, Ray silent and brooding, and Todd a complete mystery. But they each accepted their assignments, and the first hurdle was cleared.

Before the meeting broke up, John mentioned that he would be spending some time today around their cubes, working on streamlining the physical environment. He could tell by the looks on their faces that it wasn't going to be a welcome intrusion.

"You mean cleaning?" asked Kiki finally.

"No, not *cleaning*," said John, a little defensively. "Just making some changes to the physical environment that will make the work flow more rapidly." He began to realize that he was more uncomfortable with this process than he had realized.

"Well, I hate my chair," said Ray gruffly. It was the first thing he had said during the meeting.

Todd snorted. "I don't think where you sit has anything to do with the work flow," he said, laughing. "But, then again, since I've seen some of your code, maybe it does."

Ray opened his mouth to object, but John held up a hand. "I'll keep that in mind, Ray," John said. And the meeting was adjourned.

By midmorning, John had made some progress. By offering to buy them doughnuts, he had persuaded the hardware guys to clear all the old equipment out of the cubes adjacent to their team. *Food talks,* he thought to himself. He also had mounted a large Gantt chart of the new schedule on the empty wall outside the cube bank, where everyone could see it.

Kiki caught the spirit and mentioned a program that would help them keep track of where each module of code was at all times. "You'll know who's working on what, and so will we," she said. "I could look into how much it would cost," she volunteered. John was grateful for the suggestion.

The two things that were the source of the most wasted time became obvious very quickly: Ray actually *did* need a new chair, and Kiki desperately needed a new computer. John had never spent much time near his employee's work spaces before, but, from where he was most of the morning, he could see into Ray's cube. His chair was a disaster. Ray had duct-taped additional lumbar support to the back. As he worked, he shifted uncomfortably. And he required frequent breaks, moving stiffly out of his chair and down the hall.

"He has a bad back," said Kiki, noticing John watching Ray walk away toward the break room. "He had surgery last year." She held up her coffee cup. "I'll be back in a minute. I'm just waiting for my computer to reboot."

Over the course of the morning, Kiki rebooted her computer once more. John winced as he heard the beeps indicating another crash just after lunch. Deciding not to waste any time, he got on the phone with purchasing and started the requisition process.

In the afternoon, he met with Blake, to hear how the meeting with Ramon and Tracy had gone. "Really, it's a process of addition by elimination," said Blake. "Actually, I think we've scheduled in too much time to make the adjustments; it just shouldn't take that long. But we can adjust things as we go."

It was a great day, and John couldn't wait to talk to his dad, but he was taking Stephanie to a musical that night to celebrate her birthday and only had time to make a quick stop before picking her up.

Stopping at the flower stand, John noticed a man and woman at a nearby bus stop, speaking in sign language. John had taken a course in American Sign Language (ASL) in high school. He hadn't done very well, at the time he had been much more interested in the cute girls in the class. However, even then he had been impressed by the economy of words. Unlike spoken language, where there might be five different words to express the same thing, everything in ASL was stripped down to the bare necessities of communication.

Just for kicks, he tried to decipher what the man was saying with his hands, but his concentration was broken as the bus screeched to a stop and the doors hissed open. John turned back to the flowers. If only choosing flowers were simpler, more streamlined, more like sign language. He always felt stymied by the complexity of making this particular decision.

He was reaching for a bouquet of red roses (always a safe bet) when it hit him: *That's what good business is all about: stripping your product down to the bare necessities of what your customer values. Mentec wants us to understand what they value and they want us to give it to them in the least amount of time, with the least amount of resources, in the most effective way. That's Value Centered Management.*

Give it to them in the least amount of time, with the least amount of resources, in the most effective way.

It just made so much sense. He bought the flowers and got back into his car. "This is going to work," he said out loud to himself as he turned the corner. He could see the path to success and somehow that changed everything. The city lights seemed brighter. The musical was more enjoyable than he had expected (as a general rule, he wasn't a fan). John hadn't realized before how much his personal life had been affected by his frustration at work.

"That wasn't half bad," John said, as they left the theater, arm in arm.

Stephanie looked up at him and laughed. "I don't know what's up with you tonight," she said, "but I like it."

CHAPTER 4

When's the Last Time I Had My Heart Checked?

Culture: *The Seven Commitments of Value-Centered Organizations*

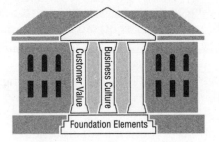

The week went by in a blur, with John continuing to look for ways to streamline their work. There were simple fixes at first: He moved the group's printer to a location just outside the cubes, so they didn't have to apply for a passport just to pick up a printout. He also obtained access to some legacy code, which saved Kiki and Ray valuable hours seeking approvals. Perhaps the most interesting change occurred on Thursday just before lunch.

"What's this?" he'd asked when Todd dropped a stack of papers onto his desk.

"The weekly," Todd said over his shoulder, as he continued to walk out of the room.

"Hey, Todd, hold up a moment," said John. Todd stopped and turned slowly, a flat expression on his face.

"What?" he asked in a monotone.

"Who asked for these reports?"

"Huh?" Todd asked, temporarily losing his studied nonchalance.

"I said, who asked you to do these reports? Cheryl? I mean, I'm willing to be wrong, but I looked at them last week, and I can't see how they help me." John flipped through the pages quickly. "There must be a couple dozen ways of looking at our system usage in here. Who originally requested them and why? And why did they ask you to do it? You're graphics?"

Todd looked stumped. "I . . . I don't know," he said, finally. "The guy I replaced was doing them, and so I did them, too. No one ever said anything about them before."

Todd and John looked at each other in surprise for a moment. Then John smiled. "For now, then, let's assume we don't need them, okay? If we find out we're wrong, can we go back and pull up the data later?"

Todd nodded.

"So, does that work for you?" asked John.

As he watched, Todd recovered his detached attitude. "Whatever you say, General," said Todd, saluting. He did a quick two-point turn and strode stiffly out of the room.

"Well, that went well," said John, wryly, staring after him.

This latest exchange was just one more reminder of a persistent problem. Even though the work was starting to flow more smoothly, personality problems were becoming more of an issue. *Or maybe just more apparent,* John thought to himself. He would have to address it soon, especially with Todd and Ray, but also with Kiki. She was so unassuming that it was difficult to get a read on her abilities. *And with Ray running constant interference . . .*

He glanced at the clock. It was lunchtime, and he was headed to Stan's for a much needed haircut.

Stan's was an old shop on Tenth Street, wedged between a Pakistani rug store and an alternative bookstore. It was old, with a faded, striped barber pole outside. Stephanie hated everything about the place, but John liked that a haircut was still just ten dollars, and that you could get an old-fashioned shave. Most of all, he never felt like a number there. The familiar bell on its dirty, knotted string jingled as he opened the door and walked in.

"Hey, guys," he said.

Two men in their seventies raised their eyes and smiled. Moe and Ed were standing in their regular spots behind two identical black vinyl barber chairs, each busily cutting a customer's hair. Around the room, several freshly trimmed customers lingered over a cup of coffee, enjoying the conversation, in no apparent hurry to leave.

"You know what?" said John. "I'm in the mood for a really lousy cup of coffee."

"Then you've come to the right place," growled Moe.

Stan walked into the room, wearing a white smock and carrying a mug of shaving cream and an old-fashioned razor.

"Did I hear you complaining about my coffee?" he asked John in mock irritation.

"That stuff is lousy," said Ed.

"So I've heard," said Stan. "You'll be glad to hear that I took your advice, and ordered that new blend you recommended. It'll be here Monday."

Around the room, the customers erupted in a cheer.

Stan seated John in an empty chair and began to cut. Around John, the barber shop was filled with the low hum of conversation and clicking scissors. He closed his eyes and relaxed, enjoying the comfortable rhythm of the ambient sounds. Slowly, he became aware of raised voices. Moe and Ed were engaging in one of their occasional arguments.

"Moe, will you go grab some towels?" asked Stan. "We're out." Moe left, grumbling under his breath.

"Okay, looks like you're all set," Stan said to John, taking off the cape and shaking it to his side, like a matador.

John stood and stretched. "They just don't make them like you anymore, Stan," he said, handing him a few bills. "Keep the change." Stan put them in an unlocked metal safe in the counter drawer without counting them.

Stan nodded and waved John out the door without ceremony.

On his way back to the office, John thought about Stan and the guys at the barbershop. They each had their own personality flaws, yet Stan handled them all so well. He remembered back a couple years ago when Ed had begun making noise about the barber chairs being ripped and broken. *They had been pretty bad,* John had to admit.

So, Stan had put Ed in charge of pricing new chairs and had purchased the chairs that Ed recommended. *He gave Ed ownership of the problem,* thought

John. Now, if anyone said anything about the chairs, Ed was the first to defend them. He also was impressed by how Stan had intercepted the escalating conflict between Ed and Moe today.

Everyone has problem personalities at work, he thought. *Some leaders just manage them better.*

Everyone has problem personalities at work. Some leaders just manage them better.

As the light turned green, John made up his mind. *I want to be one of those leaders,* he thought. And he knew just how to begin: He'd go back to his parent's house this weekend and see if his dad had any insight into handling attitude problems at work. He fished his cell phone out of his pocket and dialed the familiar number. *If I keep this up, I might have to put Dad on speed dial,* he though with a wry smile.

When John saw Stephanie later that night, she was pleased with his haircut, but disappointed when John told her he was heading out for another weekend with his parents.

"I'd like to see the house and catch up with your mom," she said. "It's been a long time."

John didn't register her comment; he was a million miles away. As Stephanie set the salad on the table, where the stack of books used to be, he said, "I just don't know what to do about the attitudes at work. You wouldn't believe the stuff that goes on there."

"Oh, yes, I would," said Stephanie, sitting down next to him. "Remember Meg, at the ad agency, who used to call home at lunch and loudly ask her housekeeper to put the dogs on the phone so she could talk to them?"

"Yeah, that was weird," he admitted. "But this is more than just having a little idiosyncrasy; this is affecting the way people perform and interact with each other."

Stephanie looked at him for a moment, then smiled mischievously. "Well, it's a good thing we're perfectly well adjusted," she said, lifting her eyebrows. "I mean, it's good that we don't worry too much or obsess endlessly about work or something annoying like that."

John paused for a moment with his fork raised above his salad, looking at her.

Stephanie laughed. "I'm teasing," she said. "Really, you know I live and breathe my work, too, so I understand. I'm just saying that maybe attitude isn't something you can fix. Maybe it's just something you have to accept and work around. Everyone has something about them that drives other people crazy.

"I mean, look at all the progress you've already made. Mentec is happier because you actually understand where they are coming from. Your project is back on schedule. Isn't that enough?"

"Maybe . . ." John said, slowly. The truth was, he wanted more than anything for Stephanie to be right. He wasn't a coward, but, given the choice, he'd rather have all his teeth pulled without anesthesia than address Todd's indifference and Ray's anger.

All night, he mulled over the problem. He'd put it off this long. Perhaps he could work around the attitude problems. Maybe he could adjust to them, or maybe he could ignore them and skirt the issue entirely.

Or maybe I could quit tiptoeing around the elephant in the room and deal with the attitude problems head on, he thought, finally, long after he had gone to bed. *Maybe it would make room for some more progress.*

Quit tiptoeing around the elephant in the room and deal with the attitude problems head on.

John left right after work on Friday, but it was dark when he pulled up to his parent's house. Despite the long drive, which usually relaxed him, he still felt keyed up. He hesitated near the front steps, then turned and walked around to the back of the house and stood on the dock in the darkness. He just needed a few minutes alone to unwind.

"Relaxing, isn't it," asked a deep voice from not far away.

John jumped and quickly scanned the beach for the source of the voice. As his eyes adjusted to the dark, he saw his dad leaning on a mooring pole.

"I was starting to wonder if you were coming out this weekend, after all," he said. "I like to sit out here before bed. It helps me relax."

Tim walked up the deck. He and John stood together in silence for a moment, watching the dark water.

"Dad, what's the next pillar?" John asked suddenly, turning toward him. "Driving out here, I started to think I might have an idea. I think it's Attitude," he said, pulling the crumpled drawing out of his pocket. "I've gone as far as I can at AXD without addressing the attitude problems," he said.

Tim was clearly pleased. "The second pillar is actually *Culture*," he said. "But attitude is a big part of it, really. And I discovered the same thing you have. After a while, if you don't address attitude, then you can't move forward."

He clapped John on the shoulder in a congratulatory way.

"Let's go inside for now," he said. "Your mom saved you a bit of supper; are you hungry?" John nodded. He suddenly felt starved; although food sounded good, he was even hungrier for answers.

Over reheated chicken enchiladas, Tim started into a lecture on culture.

"Culture is the heart of a business," said Tim. "It's what pumps the blood of success throughout the organization. It can be either the silent destroyer of a company or the silent glue that keeps a company together."

John's breath caught in his throat as he recalled an article from the morning paper: A college basketball player had died in the middle of a game. There had been no warning signs; he had appeared vibrant and healthy—just as a company might look on the outside. And, yet, if things weren't right on the inside. . . .

Tim added, "When your culture is strong, your organization can respond to change—I like to say that it can turn on a dime while still leaving your customers a quarter."

"Come again?" John laughed.

"I mean that you can respond to the ever-changing needs of your customers while still increasing value along the way." His dad looked at him with concern. "This isn't a new concept to you, is it?" he asked. John shook his head.

"No, no. I'm with you," John said.

"But what *is* new is the idea that you can actually shape team member attitudes and corporate culture," his dad continued.

"That's not new. I think every executive starts out believing that," said John. "It's what they teach you in school."

"Most leaders get discouraged early on because they expect good attitudes to come naturally, and they don't. Not hardly. They expect to write out their vision of the culture, put it on a poster, and have it play out in team members' daily business decisions. And, of course, it doesn't."

"Fair enough, but what should leaders do differently?" asked John, leaning forward in his chair. *This is going to be good,* he thought. *This is going to be brilliant.*

"You talk about attitude up front with team members. You sit down and explain to each person what is expected. You ask them to commit to demonstrating certain attitudes every day at work."

As Tim spoke, John felt an intense letdown, like he had just scaled a mountain to sit at a guru's feet, only to find simple platitudes offered. *He can't be serious,* John thought. *It's just too naïve to believe that telling your people that you want them to be better employees will make them behave that way.*

Tim didn't appear to notice John's doubts. He pulled the drawing of the house toward him and wrote Culture in the second pillar. On the back, he wrote:

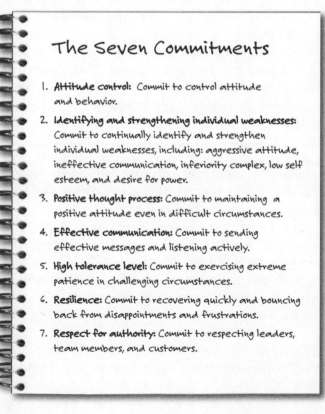

The Seven Commitments

1. **Attitude control:** Commit to control attitude and behavior.

2. **Identifying and strengthening individual weaknesses:** Commit to continually identify and strengthen individual weaknesses, including: aggressive attitude, ineffective communication, inferiority complex, low self esteem, and desire for power.

3. **Positive thought process:** Commit to maintaining a positive attitude even in difficult circumstances.

4. **Effective communication:** Commit to sending effective messages and listening actively.

5. **High tolerance level:** Commit to exercising extreme patience in challenging circumstances.

6. **Resilience:** Commit to recovering quickly and bouncing back from disappointments and frustrations.

7. **Respect for authority:** Commit to respecting leaders, team members, and customers.

"These are the seven commitments each team member should make with a coach—"

"A coach?" asked John.

"Well, you'd say supervisor, but we call them coaches because, within a Value-Centered Enterprise, coaches focus on developing people and skills, instead of being superior to someone else and exercising control. Coaching requires more energy than supervising, which is why it's so neglected.

"Anyway, if a coach takes the time to discuss these commitments with team members, it benefits them both in several ways. First, the team members develop skills that can prepare them to better handle difficult situations—even outside work. Also, it opens up communication between a leader and members of his team." he said.

"Say a team member is having trouble with maintaining a positive thought process. If the coach has talked to the team member and committed her to demonstrate the seven commitments in her work, then he can pull that person aside and say, 'You remember when you committed to demonstrate a positive attitude? We talked about how before a person can act right, she has to think right, and, well, it seems like you're having difficulty holding up part of that promise. Let's talk about it.'"

"Dad, I just don't know," said John, tipping back on the rear legs of the chair. "I—" but a childhood memory interrupted his thoughts and he bolted back upright. How many times had his mother told him that tipping onto the back legs would break the chair? And this was one of her new chairs. He felt relieved she hadn't seen him.

Watching this, his dad laughed. "You don't think talking regularly about what is expected influences behavior?" he said. "I'd say your mother got her expectations across pretty clearly with your chair tipping."

John couldn't help but grin, although he wasn't sure this was an accurate example. *How many leaders send their employees to timeout to reinforce their point?* he thought cynically. Although, on second thought, time-out didn't sound like such a bad idea after all.

The next day was busier than John had expected. For most of the afternoon, John helped his dad with chores around the house. Kneeling on the front lawn, up to their elbows in mud, fixing a sprinkler pipe, he finally brought up the question that had been nagging him since their conversation the night before.

"Dad, when you talked about attitude control last night—Well, I just don't know that a person can be in control of his attitude all the time. Is that even realistic?"

Tim didn't miss a beat. "Sure it is," he said. "Hey, hand me that wrench, would you?" John handed the mud-coated tool to him. "Thanks. Now hold this together while I tighten it."

While he worked, Tim explained. "Just think about the times you've been pulled over for speeding. You're not happy about it, that's for sure, but you control your attitude when you're talking with the police officer, hoping he will let you off. In that situation, being nice is in your best interest, and you know it.

"By explaining to a team member that it's in her best interest to exercise that same control at work— better for her if she wants to be promoted or get a raise, better for her relationship with her colleagues, and so on—a coach is doing a team member a huge service.

"There, we're almost done," Tim said, tugging one last time on the wrench.

"Actually, I don't think attitude control is the hardest commitment. I think the hardest one is strengthening our weaknesses, because we don't want to see them," said Tim, rocking back on his heels and wiping the sweat from his cheek with his forearm, smearing a line of dirt across his face. "We don't want to admit that we've got a problem with an aggressive attitude, an unhealthy desire for power, or an inferiority complex. Not only that, sometimes our greatest strengths can be our greatest weaknesses."

John cocked his head in confusion.

"Think of the gifted coaches you know who are good leaders but just can't follow. They're terrible at taking direction and coaching themselves. Or the people who are great self-starters but can't get along in a group. Their lack of balance has caused them to excel in one area, but it's also caused a deficiency in another. That can be hard to correct," said Tim.

Tim glanced over at his wife, who had stooped over to pull up a sprig of wild rosemary. "We planted just one mint plant last year. One," Tim said for emphasis, holding up a gloved index finger. "We didn't know it would go crazy, springing up everywhere. It's almost impossible to get rid of now. That's a lot like culture. You've got to be careful what you plant, careful what you nurture, because once it gets established, it's going to spread all over the organization. The Seven Commitments help guarantee you plant the right seeds."

Tim got up slowly and grabbed a shovel. "Let's get this filled in and then get cleaned up. I think we'll have a little bit of time for fishing off the dock before dinner if we're quick."

John picked up the shovel and started filling in the hole.

Before John realized it, it was dinnertime. He hadn't realized how hungry he was until he walked into the house and got a whiff of cherry pie, straight from the oven.

Bringing it to the table at the end of the meal, his mom cut John a piece double the size of the other two. Falling back into the habits of his teens, he took an oversized bite—and immediately rushed to the garbage can to spit it out. His mother was shocked.

"John! What in the world?" she asked, astounded. She took a tiny piece of the pie and nibbled at it tentatively.

"Oh, my goodness! Double salt! Tim, don't eat it," she warned, pulling his plate away. "I was going to double the recipe and then decided against it. I must have doubled the salt anyway," she said.

"Oooh, I'm so sorry, John," she said, dumping the pie in the trash.

For a moment, everyone stared mournfully at the trash can. Then, John had an idea.

"Hey, why don't I treat you two to pie down at Spinners?" he asked, grinning. His parents agreed. While his mother changed, John and his father waited at the table.

"You know, that mistake with the pie made me think about something with culture," his dad said. "Your mom couldn't have timed it better, although she'd kill me for saying that." He put a finger in front of his lips in a secretive gesture.

"You know, in order to give your customers what they value, your culture has to have the right ingredients," he said. "Or you'll end up with all your efforts in the trash," he said, smiling.

"Attitude control is one thing. We talked about that," Tim said, ticking it off with his fingers. "*Kaizen* is another."

"Kaizen? Never heard of it," said John.

"In the Japanese language, *kai* means 'change' and *zen* means 'for the better.' So, Kaizen means 'a change for the better;' and it takes continuous improvement to the next level. With continuous improvement, supervisors create an environment in which improvement is welcome. In Kaizen, coaches actually train team members to spot areas that can be improved and give them the ability to implement and control the improvement process themselves," he said. "Coaches who initiate Kaizen actually expect team members to make improvements as part of their jobs. And that makes all the difference in the world. Can you think why?"

John thought about it. He remembered all the times, even as a manager, where he'd thought of a good idea, but had been put off by all the red tape he'd have to go through to get it implemented. It was easier to just let things ride, to go with the status quo. He nodded.

"So many good ideas die in the red tape," John said.

"Right. That's why it's so important to go further than continuous improvement and develop cultural improvement systems that embed improvement into the very DNA of your team. With Kaizen, implementing improvement isn't an *activity* but an *environment*."

Tim stopped as he heard his wife's footsteps on the stairs. "Well, let's go," he said. "We can talk later. I'll drive, you pay."

On the way to the restaurant, John shared his memory of the bobble-head dolls on his Grandma Rose's dashboard. His mom smiled.

"I used to look for fun new bobble heads to bring her from wherever we went on vacation," she said. "By the way, did Dad tell you that we're heading to Florida in a couple of weeks?" his mom asked.

"It's part of a training seminar for my team," said his dad, proudly. "Remind me to tell you about it later. I think you'll find it interesting."

"Maybe I'll look for a bobble head to bring to you as a present, John," his mother said, smiling.

John grimaced and she laughed. "Then again, maybe not."

At the restaurant, John waited until the pie had been served to ask his dad about the training.

"Well, every year, I ask all my managers what training they would most value during the coming year. Some years they all ask for different types of training. This year, they all seemed to be interested in one thing. So, we're heading down to Florida together for a few days."

"Surfing training?" John asked.

Tim smiled. "No, actually, this training focuses on aligning team members with what they do best. Most coaches aren't good at that, because they don't listen, so they don't know what their team members are best at or what they enjoy. Oh, I could go on forever about that," Tim said. "But I won't," he added quickly, glancing at his wife, who was giving him a stern look.

"What you'll find interesting, John, is that leadership development is a huge deal if you want to create a healthy culture."

"You know, my group is so small, I'm the only leader," said John.

"Oh, that's where you're wrong," said Tim. "There are several levels of leadership and, ultimately, all team members need to be transformed into some type of leader, even if it just means learning how to lead themselves to do the right things on a daily basis. Your job as their coach is to get them to all think like CEOs, taking full responsibility for their work."

John hadn't thought of that.

"Next on my list for a healthy culture is very close to what we've been talking about." He glanced at his wife, who was making a time-out signal with her hands. "I know," he said apologetically. "I'll stop. Just one more quick thing," he said.

"Team member development is vital. Don't expect your team members to demonstrate outstanding performance without investing in outstanding development systems for them. An underdeveloped team will lead to underdeveloped service for your customers.

"It's important to train team members in job skills, but just as important to teach them life skills. People spend up to 80 percent of their lives at work," said Tim, drawing a large heart on a napkin and making notations around it. As he did it, he glanced nervously at Linda, who was patiently listening to the lecture:

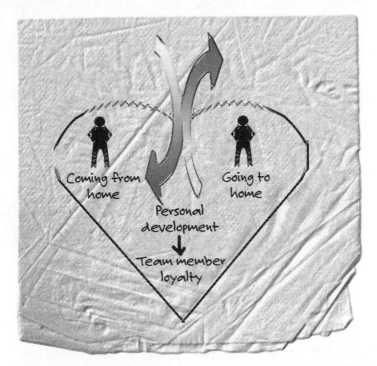

"If team members are out of whack at home, that will filter into the workplace, affecting the customer," said Tim, drawing arrows. "So, effective coaches teach personal skills, too—like money management, organizational skills, or even arrange ESL classes. And they end up with more effective, more loyal, team members. Why do you think that's so?"

"Because they're not just putting up with you for the money. Their life is better because of their employment," answered John.

Tim nodded. "There, now, I'm done." He winked at his wife.

"Promise no more shoptalk for the rest of the night?" she said.

"Whenever you're around, our lips are sealed," said John.

"But all bets are off when you're not," said Tim.

At that point, all conversation was drowned out by a live band, making it impossible for anyone to talk about anything. John didn't mind. He enjoyed the next hour, sitting out in the open air, watching the dinner crowd, salsa music filling the air.

Leaving the restaurant, they walked lazily to the door, following a large family. A teenaged boy exited the restaurant ahead of his grandmother, who followed slowly, hobbling on a cane. Without thinking, he let go of the door, and the woman was knocked backward into John.

"Are you okay?" John asked, helping the woman regain her balance and holding the door open until she was safely outside. Embarrassed, the woman thanked him and hobbled as quickly as possible in the direction of the car.

"Respect. It's not taught anymore, really," said Tim, sadly. "It's no wonder it's so difficult to ensure that customers get the respect they deserve from team members."

John nodded soberly, and then brightened as an idea crossed his mind. "Hey, why don't we take a walk along the beach in the morning?" he asked. "Maybe we could find that place with all the tidal pools that I always loved."

His mom and dad didn't need a second invitation.

"That place is too far up the beach to walk to; I'd say it's at least five miles," his dad said. "We could take the boat. We'll just have to fill it up first."

They all awoke early the next morning. The sun was just cresting over the low hills when they tied the boat up at the filling station. A kid with a dark brown tan, bare feet, and a nose stud strode out to meet them.

"Good to see you," he said, without making eye contact. John almost laughed at the irony between his words and body language. How could it possibly be good to see them when he clearly hadn't even looked at them?

"Fill it?" he asked. Tim nodded, looking analytically at the kid.

"This guy is classic," said his dad in a low voice.

When John looked at him in a confused way, he said, "Customer service is on my list for building a healthy culture. This kid is confusing customer service with lip service, and it shows."

Eventually the young guy turned and told them the total. Tim handed over his credit card and waited for him to return.

"Five bucks says he thanks us for coming by today, but he doesn't even crack a smile when he says it," said his father.

As if on cue, the boy walked out and handed Tim a credit card and receipt.

"Thank you for letting us serve you today," he said, barely finishing the sentence before turning his back on them and walking away.

"Wow. I'm underwhelmed," said John.

"Of course, just because you make a person say 'Have a nice day' doesn't mean you are great at customer service. Neither is just a smile and an appearance of happiness while serving your customers. It goes deeper than that—understanding what your customer values and taking the time to center all operations, policies, procedures, and behaviors within the organization around that value.

"I came up with a way to keep this at the forefront of my mind," said his dad, settling back into the boat. He waited as John climbed in, and said, "It's KIND."

"What's kind?" asked John, swinging around to scan the boat and the dock.

"No, it's K-I-N-D," said Tim, laughing a little. He grabbed an envelope from his bag and wrote:

Keep the client satisfied.

Initiate communication and feedback.

Never leave a client disappointed.

Deliver on all promises.

"When you told me about the woman you replaced; what's her name?"

"Cheryl."

"Right, when you told me about Cheryl's last meeting with Mentec, I could see a problem right away," said Tim. "She left the client disappointed, by telling them that since AXD was meeting the specs, they weren't going to make any more changes."

"I see that now," said John. "And because of that, we almost lost the contract."

"But did you see how quickly they responded when you initiated communication and feedback? It was night and day," said Tim. "That's the power of KIND."

"Speaking of power," John's mom said from behind them. "I'm thinking we'd better power up the boat or we'll never get to the tidal pools."

"You're a taskmaster, mom," said John, then asked, "Hey, Dad, mind if I drive? It's been a while."

His dad waved him on and went to sit down next to his wife.

John pulled the boat smoothly out of dock. As their speed increased, John thought how good it felt to be moving so quickly. And how much he enjoyed taking the wheel.

Leadership should feel like this, he thought, enjoying the feeling of sea spray in his face. *A good leader builds up his team members and creates the right culture so that when the course is chosen, everyone is revved and ready to go.*

A good leader builds up his team members and creates the right culture so that when the course is chosen, everyone is revved and ready to go.

He urged the boat forward even faster. *With the right culture, I can take our team anywhere,* he thought. He could hardly wait for Monday.

Monday started out like any other, with the managers' meeting first on the docket. John was looking forward to reporting in; he had good things to say. So, he was taken by surprise when Mike reacted negatively.

"You say you've been sending Blake to meet with Mentec? Why haven't marketing and sales been involved?" he asked, shortly.

John was taken aback. Was Mike feeling threatened? Now that he thought about it, he could see how he might. He had been intimately involved with the Mentec deal when Cheryl was heading the project.

"We haven't been in sales mode," said John, trying to explain. "The meetings have involved making changes to the product that they requested; Blake is uniquely qualified for that."

"This isn't how we've done things in the past. We've always been the liaison with the client," said Mike, stiffly. However, he let the subject drop.

Kaye jumped in. "Anyway, I'm pleased to see you're back on schedule," she said. "But what happened with the speed-reading seminar? That was a corporate initiative. HR said your team bowed out at the last minute, and I took some flak."

John nodded. What could he say? "With our tight deadline, and Mentec such a critical client, I felt we couldn't spare the time for the seminar right now." *Or ever,* he added to himself.

She nodded coldly, and the meeting moved on, leaving John slightly dazed. When it ended, he stood to leave, anxious to get back and hear how Blake's meeting with Mentec had gone. But Kaye asked him to stay.

After waiting for the room to clear she said, "Go ahead and sit back down, John. I want to clarify my earlier remarks. Of course, I can't argue with results, and your getting the project back on track is certainly impressive. However," she paused here for emphasis, "When we said we wanted someone fearless and with youthful enthusiasm, you'll notice we didn't say we wanted a *maverick*. It's okay to think outside the box, just not too far. I'm just offering some words to the wise. That's all."

John understood he had been dismissed and left the room absolutely baffled by what had just happened. Here he was picturing his group speeding over the water toward their goal, but everyone else seemed to think he was just rocking the boat. *I'll have to be careful not to make waves for the next little bit*, he thought. *I'll just work quietly on culture.*

He had no idea how short-lived that resolution would be.

Blake was waiting in his office when he returned. He looked breathless with enthusiasm.

"I need to talk to you," he said. "I've been waiting."

John invited him to sit. Blake immediately began to speak. "I met with Mentec today. Well, you know that. I showed them the changes we've made, and they were ecstatic about them. Then we talked about the next few changes, and it just sort of naturally evolved into a discussion about getting the employees to use the software and before I knew it, we were talking about AXD providing product training when it's completed."

He stopped suddenly and looked at John, waiting for a reaction. John was speechless.

"I know it's not where we expected to go," continued Blake, almost apologetically. "But you told me to find out what Mentec values, and this is what they value right now," he said. "They want us to help get their employees trained to use this software. We wrote it, they see us as the experts, and they want us to provide the training."

John was silent.

"Mr. Jackson, from Trenneth, thinks it's a good idea," said Blake.

"Mr. Jackson?" John was shocked.

"Well, he was there when I arrived, and Ramon invited him to join the meeting because what we're doing affects warehousing. By the way, he loved the changes, too. And he was very enthusiastic about the training idea. He wants to be involved with that."

John struggled to collect his thoughts. This was fabulous and horrific. Fabulous because Blake had hit on a new revenue stream from Mentec. They were asking AXD to take their money. Practically begging. *Just like Dad said they would if we found what they value,* thought John.

However, he had to consider his conversation with Kaye. How would this look when he reported back? "Oh, by the way, we're now going to provide training, something AXD has never done before." He had a sinking feeling the reaction wouldn't be entirely positive. Hadn't he just told Mike they weren't in sales mode? Hadn't Kaye said they didn't want a maverick?

This will take some thought. For now, though, I need to reassure Blake that he's on the right track.

"Blake, I'm overwhelmed. You've really taken this assignment and run with it. Who would have thought you'd not only help save the old contract, but bring in a potential new revenue stream, too? Give me some time to think about it. We'll talk in the morning. But good work," he said.

Blake nodded. He seemed to be satisfied with John's answer.

"I'll follow up with Kiki and Ray on the next round of changes," he said. John thanked him, and he was soon left alone with his thoughts. Just then, a pop-up box indicated a new e-mail. As an out from his current worries, he opened up his mail and found a quick note from his dad.

"Last night I wanted to share this with you, but ran out of time. It's always helped me. Love, Dad." Below was a list:

LEAD

Lead the company in the right direction. (Even if it's not popular.)

Encourage others to maintain the vision. (Support their innovative efforts.)

Add intrinsic value to the organization (Do the things that build value in ways you can't see, like building up a team member.)

Deliver management support at all times (No team member should be under your leadership who doesn't get the support they need. Whatever the problems, a leader needs to deliver.)

Talk about perfect timing, John thought. The answer is that I've got to continue to LEAD. Immediately, as if by instinct, John pulled out the drawing of the house and smoothed it flat on his desk:

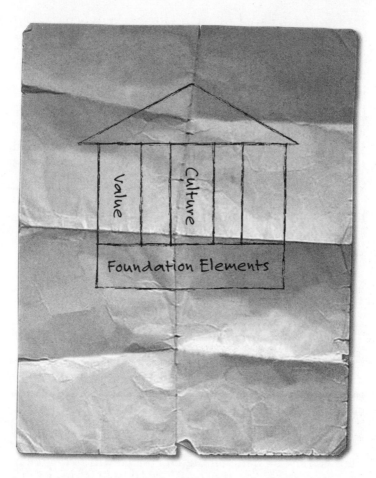

It's all coming together, he thought, *his finger tracing the foundation.* We've begun to streamline our operations, which has freed Blake to be our Value-Management professional. And now, Mr. Jackson has joined our Customer Value Committee. *His finger moved to the Value pillar.* We've made real progress changing the code to deliver what Mentec values, and now we've found this new revenue stream.

He remembered his dad saying, "The best situation is to find a new revenue stream that doesn't cost you anything."

He didn't know if that was possible in this case. Wouldn't he have to hire a trainer? How much could he charge? Would he have to create training materials and workbooks?

His finger moved to Culture. He had planned to start working on that today; but everything had changed.

He sensed someone looking at him and looked up to see Todd standing in the doorway. Only there was something different about him, something in his eyes. Was it excitement?

"Hey, I overheard Blake talking about Mentec possibly wanting us to provide training. Is it true?"

Oh, no, John thought. *I thought Blake understood not to talk about it yet.*

"It's on the table, although we haven't decided where to go with it yet," said John.

"That's why I want to talk to you," said Todd, coming into the office. "I think there's something about me you should know."

Todd had a teaching degree. It was too much to believe. After sitting down with John, he had explained how he had completed college with a degree in education, but right out of school had followed the money into the software industry instead.

"I do graphics because I'm good at it, and it pays the bills," he said. "But teaching—or training—is what I really want to do," he said. "I think I can do both here at AXD. I spend a lot of time coasting."

For a moment, Todd looked scared, as if he hadn't meant to reveal that.

"I'm just asking for a shot at the training position," he said, looking John straight in the eye.

John seized the opportunity.

"I would love to see that work out for you. But we're just in the preliminary stages of this, so I can't guarantee anything at this point. Right now, I want to establish some expectations about your attitude here at work that will help open doors for you."

Todd nodded his head, "I know I've been—"

"That's ancient history, as far as I'm concerned. I'm talking about today forward. There are seven commitments I want you to make with me today, Todd, concerning the way you go about your work, starting right now, with what you're doing with the graphics."

John paused and took one more look at the crumpled paper on his desk, his index finger still pointing at the Culture box. He was on the brink of something, the point of no return, maybe? Did he really want to get this deep into Value-Centered Management?

He hesitated for a moment, considering. Then he took one hard look at the sincere expression on Todd's face and made up his mind. He took a deep breath and dove in.

The rest of the conversations went better than he could have hoped. Blake was instantly responsive. And during his meeting with Kiki, John was able to address his suspicion that she was underutilized.

"On identifying individual weaknesses," John said to her. "I think you could take a larger role on this project than you are currently. I think you can do more than we're letting you do here. Am I right?"

Kiki looked down at the floor as she spoke. "I don't mind. Ray enjoys being in charge, and I just like to code." She looked up suddenly. "You're not saying you think I'm trying to avoid responsibility, are you?"

"No." said John firmly. "Absolutely not. I'm saying I think we've made a mistake by not allowing you to demonstrate your full abilities."

"Well, I admit that I wouldn't mind stretching my wings a little," she said, shyly.

"Well, you've committed to strengthening your weaknesses, as part of the Seven Commitments. Can I count on you to be ready when I call on you to step up?"

Kiki pulled her eyes away from her hands in her lap.

"Yes," she said with conviction. And from where he sat, John could sense her resolve.

After Kiki left the room, John looked up at the clock. Four o'clock. It would be tight, but he could still call Ray in and talk to him, even if they needed to finish the meeting in the morning. That would be the right thing to do. And he would do it, too, if it weren't for a couple of important calls he needed to make now.

It really is too bad, he thought as he dialed the first number. *I really did want to get all the meetings done today.*

Even as he thought it, he knew it was a lie.

CHAPTER 5

Lean Management Is for Manufacturing, Right? Wrong.

Flow: *Don't Work Faster, Make Work Move Faster*

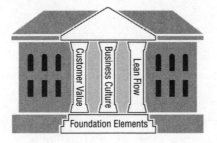

Early the next morning, John was just climbing out of his car, juggling his briefcase and a couple of folders with loose papers, when his cell rang. He fished the phone out of his pocket and answered it.

"Hey, John!"

Automatically, in response to his father's booming voice, John moved the phone several inches away from his ear.

"I'm coming up to the city today for an appointment. You want to go to lunch?"

This was unusual. Tim's job rarely required him to come to the city on business. And was that a staple gun he heard in the background?

"That would be great, Dad. Where do you want to meet?"

"Actually, I was thinking maybe we could get some takeout and head back to your apartment. I have something to talk over with you."

John was intrigued. "Sounds fine. I'll grab something on the way home and meet you there at noon. That sound okay?"

"Huh? What do you need, Linda?" he heard his dad ask. "Hold on, your mom wants to say something."

"John?" Linda's voice came on the line. "Don't keep him too late, okay? I know how you two are when you start talking business, but it's a long drive, and your dad needs to be back before it gets too dark. He can't see at night to drive."

In the background, he heard his dad arguing that he could see just fine at night. Their voices echoed slightly, like they were in a large, empty room. *Like the garage?* John wondered.

"I've got work to do, Mom. I'll boot him out before too long," he said.

He could hear his parents' muffled voices as the phone was exchanged again.

"I'll see you at noon, then, I guess" said his dad, sounding slightly harried. "Your mom worries too much, you know."

"It's hard taking care of someone as cantankerous as you," said John.

His dad laughed. "I guess that's probably true."

And, without another word, the line went dead.

Several hours later, John found himself stuck in traffic. He had decided to postpone his meeting with Ray again, in hopes that the time with his dad would give him inspiration. Still, several minor crises had kept him at the office longer than he had planned and then he had run into traffic.

He glanced at the clock on his dashboard: 11:45 A.M. *I should have taken the I-90,* he thought, tapping his fingers on the steering wheel. He was on edge; he still needed to pick up the food, and his dad would be waiting.

He checked the clock again. 11:46. *Am I stuck in a time warp?*

According to the traffic report on the radio, a delivery truck had collided with an SUV, spilling pastries all over the expressway. It would have been funny, if he weren't stuck in it. He flipped the radio off and called his dad's cell phone. No one answered, but he left a message that he was certain his dad would not hear in time.

He suddenly realized he was grinding his teeth. *Whoa, slow down, there's nothing you can do now,* he coached himself as he inched forward.

By the time he reached the site of the collision 20 minutes later, there was nothing to see except a street crew sweeping up glass and leftover pastries as two highway patrol officers looked on. He was surprised to find only one lane of traffic closed.

Amazing how such a small thing can cause such a big pileup, he thought. As he moved past the obstruction, he opened the engine up. He was five minutes late already; he couldn't afford any more delays.

He reached his apartment with the food in hand. As he pulled up, he scanned the street for his dad, but didn't see him. *Maybe he's running a little late, too*, he thought hopefully. He avoided the elevator and took the stairs two at a time.

As he approached his door at a jog, he was surprised to see it cracked open. Getting closer, he heard voices from inside. One was Stephanie's; he recognized her laugh right away. One was his dad's.

He pushed the door open and found them in the living room with a bag of tortilla chips open on the coffee table. He didn't know how or why Stephanie had happened to be here when his dad showed up, but he was relieved and pleased to see them talking so comfortably together.

"I see you didn't hold the party up for me," he said, loudly, with a grin.

They both looked up and smiled.

"I hope you're willing to share," said Stephanie, looking at the takeout boxes. "I'm starved."

John set the boxes down on the coffee table and began to open them. "Plenty for everyone," he said. "Sorry I'm late; I was stuck in a traffic jam."

"Your dad invited me. He said you'd need my help . . . and he's been telling me a little about this Value-Centered Management that you've been so obsessed with lately," she said.

John immediately felt alarmed.

"Are you sure you have time? I thought you had a meeting with a *client*," he said, with emphasis. His eyes communicated that this was her out.

Stephanie smiled. "Oh, no, I'm in," she said. Sensing his concern, she insisted, "Really, John, I'm interested. There's no place I'd rather be."

After they had eaten, John pulled out the drawing, which was now frayed like a pirate's treasure map. He

set it down on the table amid the empty food containers. Stephanie looked at it curiously; and Tim laughed
out loud when he saw it.

"You know, it's not a Picasso. You don't have to
hang onto the original," he said. John was surprised.
He hadn't noticed how ragged it had become.

"Hey, look at how valuable the papers of other
visionaries have become," John joked, a little embarrassed that this scrap of paper had become so important to him.

Stephanie leaned closer to read the lettering within
the boxes.

Tim leaned in, too. "You see, the first pillar, Value,
is the innermost driving force that would cause a person to spend their money to buy a product or a service," he said, pointing it out to her. "The second pillar
is Culture."

"The last pillar," Tim said, looking up at John, "is
Flow."

At the word, John instinctively lifted his eyes to
the painting on the wall behind his dad's head.

"Flow is a concept that's been around in the manufacturing industry for years—only they call it *Lean.* It
was instituted by Toyota soon after World War II and
has transformed the manufacturing industry forever,"
said Tim. "A few years ago, I started wondering if similar principles could work in the service industry, for organizations like yours and mine, and discovered that,
with Value-Centered Management, they could. We call
the lean process within the service industry Flow.

"When I think of Flow, I picture my product as a
boat on a river trying to get downstream. The river is
the stream of processes and activities that deliver
what the customer values. Can you see that?"

John could. As Tim spoke, John continued to glance
now and then at the picture on the wall that had always

reminded him of a fast-flowing river. *Or maybe a stream,* he thought. *I've even imagined being carried along in the flow,* he thought, *just like Dad is saying.*

John forced himself to pull his eyes from the painting and focus on his dad's words.

"Flow is one of the most critical pillars in the Value-Centered Enterprise. It's what business is all about, because even though you may identify what your customers value, all of this does you no good if you don't properly ensure that value flows to them consistently."

Flow is one of the most critical pillars in the Value-Centered Enterprise.

"I get it," said John, a look of dawning amazement spreading over his face. "It makes so much sense. Someone values something, and a company is put together to deliver it. Everything comes down to the Value Stream."

"And the irony is that," said Tim, "within most businesses, we've got heads of marketing, heads of IT and sales, we've got executives over physical fitness, even, but who is in charge of delivering value to the client? No one."

Tim looked over his shoulder at the kitchen table, where John noticed a plastic box a few inches wide and about two feet long. Motioning toward it, Tim said, "I built something to show you what I mean about Flow."

Curious, John and Stephanie went to the table. Inside the box, were several dividers, some higher than others. One end of the box hung over the edge of the table. A hole was drilled into that end, and a bucket sat under it on the floor:

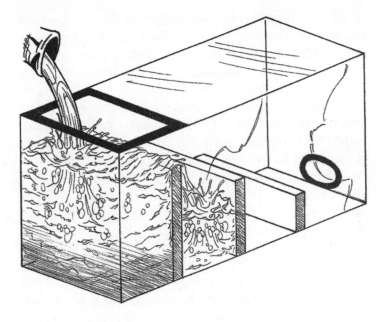

John was baffled. He looked at Stephanie, and she shrugged her shoulders to show she was just as stumped as he was.

Tim hefted a large pitcher of water.

"This box is your entire company. The water is work that needs to be completed by the company's team members. You'll know it's completed when it gets into the bucket over there on the floor. Your goal is to get as much of this work completed as you can. Go ahead. Try it." Tim thrust the pitcher into John's hands.

John began to pour the water into the end of the box opposite the hole. It took a long time for the water to top the first barrier and begin to flow toward the second—and lower—barrier. Stephanie encouraged him to pour more quickly, but it didn't increase the speed of the water flowing over the barriers by much. Finally, it was over the second barrier and flowing toward the third. The pitcher was two-thirds empty and they still hadn't reached the final barrier. John poured faster. He had emptied the bucket before the first drop of water fell into the bucket.

"This shows how people in a company may have a lot of work, but it's not flowing because there are too many inefficient processes that slow things down.

"Now imagine if you were able to pour the water into a box with little or no barriers—allowing the water to have a level flow with minimal peaks and valleys. In other words, you are reducing overburden on certain areas and underutilization on others, and you are leveling or smoothing the work and distributing it evenly. How quickly would that water—or work—be completed?"

For a moment, they all stood looking at the box. Very little of the water had made it to the end; most of it remained puddled behind the barriers.

"When work is blocked, it affects customers; they don't get what they want when they want it. It also affects employees, causing fatigue, frustration, and burnout. Sound familiar?"

Tim looked at John thoughtfully. "You're awfully quiet," he said. "Think of the traffic jam you were stuck in today. One blocked lane impacted traffic flow in all the others. Nothing went smoothly. Nothing arrived on schedule. There are blockages like that all throughout an organization, and it backs everything up.

"In contrast, Flow is focused on reducing costs by finding wasted time and resources and removing those blockages, allowing a business to operate more efficiently. And the best thing about Flow," said Tim enthusiastically, "is that wherever there is a customer who values something, and a process is needed to deliver that value, you can apply the Flow concept."

Tim turned to look at them. In a weird way, John felt like maybe they should clap. But he couldn't move. His mind was spinning, considering all the possibilities. He looked over at Stephanie. *Was she also seeing business in a whole new light?*

"I never thought of business like this before," John said lamely. Tim smiled broadly. "Focusing on the Value Stream changes how you approach everything. Here, let me show you something interesting," Tim said, grabbing an open envelope from John's counter. "Mind if I use this?" he asked.

"This is the way traditional management thinks." Tim wrote:

$$Sales\ Price = Cost + Profit$$

"And this is the way Flow forces you to think instead":

$$Sales\ Price - Cost = Profit$$

"See the difference? Within a Value-Centered Enterprise focused on Flow, profit is created by lowering costs. We do that in service organizations like ours by eliminating barriers to productivity."

"And how do you find these blockages? By observing the Value Stream?" asked Stephanie. John was always impressed by how sharp Stephanie was. He could tell his father was, too.

"Right. Each stream includes all the actions that are necessary to produce a product or service. To find them, consider yourself attached to an order or request for service and follow yourself from the point of the order until the customer is satisfied.

"Oh, and you can also map out the flow of activities within a company, to your internal customers. It works for that, too," Tim added.

"Mapping out the Value Stream takes time and, so many leaders skip it. That's a problem, because before you can decide how to improve, you need an accurate picture of where the blockages are. Thus, it's critical to take the time to visually map the flow of value-added and nonvalue-added activities within your company. That's the next step in Value-Centered Management, John."

John knew his dad was right. And already a plan was forming in his head—a way to kill two birds with one stone. He thought of Stan and Ed at the barbershop and the new chairs. He would involve Ray in mapping the Value Stream, give him ownership of it. Maybe this way, his biggest problem could become a solution to both his Flow and attitude problems.

"One more thing, and then I've got to fly," Tim said, checking his watch. "Remember way back on your first visit to the new house, John, when we talked about identifying the nonvalue-added activities in an organization? You remember, right?"

Without waiting for a reply, Tim scribbled them down again quickly on the envelope:

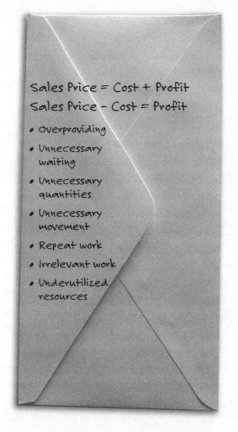

Sales Price = Cost + Profit
Sales Price - Cost = Profit

- Overproviding
- Unnecessary waiting
- Unnecessary quantities
- Unnecessary movement
- Repeat work
- Irrelevant work
- Underutilized resources

"These seven blockages can be deadly to productivity. These are the types of things mapping the Value Stream will help you discover and eliminate.

"Be especially careful about overproviding," warned Tim. "A lot of companies use a *push* system, which produces products and services with little or no regard for what is needed by the customer. What you want to have is a *pull* system, which only produces what the customer requests and needs. Remember, only the customer holds the information about when and how much you should provide."

Tim checked his watch. "I promised your mom I'd leave by three. That gives me 30 minutes to show you how to do the Value Stream Mapping. Grab a pen," Tim said to John. "And let's get started."

The next morning, John didn't even stop in at his own office before he went to Ray's cube to talk. He'd decided that Ray would be more receptive in his own space, less defensive, less on edge. At least, he hoped that's how it would go.

"Ray," he began, sitting down in the small cube. "I was hoping to get your help with something." He could tell immediately that the request had taken Ray off guard.

In the short silence, John explained how he needed someone to map out the Value Stream for their group.

"In particular, I need you to identify how long each process takes and how long code waits between those processes. I need you to map it all out on paper, including the times. You should use the other team members in gathering times and data."

"Well, I don't know," said Ray. "When do you need it? You've got us up against the wire, with Blake gone so much."

John considered before he spoke. "I know, and that's why I need your expertise. Right now, we're trying to work faster, instead of making our work *move* faster. If we can find and eliminate the activities that don't add any value, we'll have more time to do the things that really matter. That's where you come in."

Ray didn't disagree, which John viewed as encouraging. He quickly laid out the diagram his dad had made the night before.

"See, this is how it should look," John said. On the far left of the paper was a box labeled, "Specs received from customer." On the opposite end was a box labeled "Delivered to customer." John explained how Ray would need to insert boxes in between for all the processes he identified. Arrows would indicate the wait time between boxes where work just sat.

"Below each box, you should identify the time that process takes. That's called *process time.* Do the same beneath each arrow, to indicate how long the software sits before it's touched again. That's the *wait time.*"

Ray nodded, but looked skeptical. John began again, speaking a little more rapidly. He wasn't sure how much more direction Ray would tolerate, and he wanted to give him a clear and complete picture of the assignment.

"Now, it's important that you approach this with the right mindset. You've got to begin by throwing out any assumptions you might have about work flow. You'll have to go observe things firsthand and double check even the things you think you already know. You might be surprised. In fact, you might want to draw things out in pencil, because it's almost guaranteed that you'll have to change things along the way as you gather more data."

"I'm a computer guy, I'll do it on the computer," said Ray.

"Okay," said John. "Just be sure to focus on the most accurate and useful information available and let the workplace speak for itself. Involve the team, ask them questions. Oh, and don't worry about finding solutions for now. In fact, try not to even think about them. That will come later."

Ray was looking at John now, a curious expression on his face. *Does he think this is all a big joke?* wondered John. He felt anxious to leave; but instead he pressed on.

"I know this all may sound a little unusual, but it's important. There's just one more thing: If you have the time, you might want to put a description under each box outlining whatever is interesting about that process, maybe the equipment used, or quality problems if you see them. After all, you would probably be the expert on code quality," he said.

When Ray didn't acknowledge the compliment, John decided it was time to play his last card.

"Now, I know this is a lot to ask, so I'll understand if you can't handle it on top of everything else." He picked up the paper, as if to put it back in his briefcase. "You were my first choice, but I can ask Kiki or . . ."

He could tell immediately that his plan had worked.

"Well, I guess I could do it," said Ray in a growl. He took the paper from John and turned back to the computer.

"Great, Ray," said John. "I hoped you would. Just let me know if you need anything." He ducked out of the cube quickly, grateful to get out of there, but couldn't help smiling on the way back to his office. It wasn't much, but John knew progress when he saw it, and this was a huge step forward.

After their meeting, John didn't hear from Ray for more than a week, but he did see signs of progress. Once or twice, he noticed Ray with a pad of yellow legal paper in his hand (and a pencil!) looking over code with Kiki and Blake. He also found him in the break room one day, pouring over old Gantt charts from early in the project with a calculator in his hand.

John was dying to ask how things were going, but kept his distance. He figured Ray would let him know how it was going when he was ready—and it wouldn't help to push. But he thought the suspense might kill him.

On Friday, John returned home late to a dark apartment, his mind still filled with work.

"Surprise!"

John's hands clenched into fists as the lights flashed on. Stephanie laughed and rushed up to give him a kiss.

"Happy birthday!" she said. John was shocked. He had forgotten it was his birthday. In the background, he registered a festive table and a cheesecake with too many candles to count.

"I decided we needed a party—both of us, you and me. We've been working too hard, lately," she said.

Just then the phone rang, it was John's dad, "I just thought of something I forgot to tell you the other night," his dad began without introduction, apology, or even a "happy birthday."

"I wanted to tell you before we head out to Florida tomorrow. When you've got the Flow mapped out, meet with your team somewhere outside the office to discuss the blockages, like a miniretreat. Don't just do it during staff meeting. It just will deteriorate into finger-pointing."

"Gotcha," said John. "Thanks."

As he hung up the phone, Stephanie, who had been standing by his side, pulled a package out from behind her back. "I got you a present."

John opened the small box to find a small silver sculpture that looked like a house. As he looked closer, he noticed writing on the foundation, three pillars, and peaked roofline. He squinted at the pillars. They read: Value, Culture, Flow.

"Where did you get this?" he asked, shocked. "It's my—my paper," he said.

"Look at the roof," urged Stephanie. Looking closely John noticed that words filled the triangle.

"How do you know what comes next?" he asked, a little indignantly.

"Oh, I have my connections," Stephanie teased. "Okay, your dad filled me in," she admitted. "Look, the roof is the Structure and Strategy of Value-Centered Management. I've got to hand it to him, too. This stuff is addictive," Stephanie leaned back with a sigh. "I mean, I keep thinking about it all the time. It gets under your skin."

John was relieved to hear he wasn't the only one. He picked up the sculpture and read the principles of Structure and Strategy:

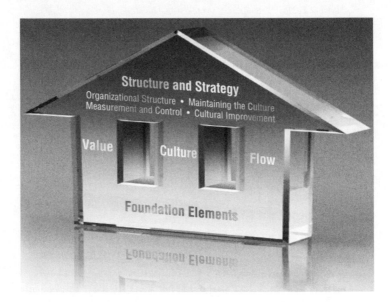

Running his finger over the engraved words, John realized how far he had come in building a Value-Centered Enterprise, and a feeling of satisfaction washed over him.

Things were going better than he could have hoped. Just that day, Ray had given him the Value Stream analysis, and it was something to celebrate.

He smiled, remembering how Ray had entered his office that morning, looking as defiant as usual.

"Here it is," Ray had said, without preface, sliding a single paper across the table. There were two charts on the sheet; one significantly longer than the other.

"The top one is how we do things now," said Ray, pointing to a box labeled Total Process Time. "The process time to get a piece of code through our system by our team is 14 business days on average."

"That's not bad," John had replied.

"No, but we can do better," Ray said. "I was surprised by how much time we waste—and where. If you divide the Total Process Time by the total time, you can see that we spend only 50 percent of our time actually working on the software. The rest is spent in wait time. And I also think we can tighten up our process time."

John was shocked; he had expected some delay, but nothing this significant. Ray pointed to the Total Process Time box underneath the shorter chart. "Seven days is all we really need, if we change a few things."

In explanation, Ray had guided him through several points along the original diagram where the code sat waiting for someone to do something to it. "We've got big wait time backups here, here and here," he said.

"One of the wait time holdups is Kiki's code waiting for review," he said. John held his breath as Ray paused. "I never realized it was such a backup," Ray said, almost to himself. Looking up at John, he said, "I think she's to a point now where she doesn't need to have her code reviewed by me . . . or anyone else."

John wanted to grin, but nodded instead.

"Tell me about the rest of the backups," he said.

John soon discovered that Ray had been thorough. *Maybe a little bit too thorough,* he thought with chagrin, when Ray brought up the last wait time issue.

"Sometimes Kiki and I sit for hours or even a full day waiting for you to give us our new assignments," said Ray. John immediately knew it was true; still, he felt a little defensive. He recovered quickly, reminding himself that Ray had overcome his pride to benefit the group. If Ray could do it, so could he.

"I know that's true," said John. "Ray, you've done an amazing job. This really could change everything. Will you present it to the group at our meeting on Monday?"

Ray agreed. As he left the room, John realized nothing had changed, and yet everything had changed. Ray's manner was still unpolished and gruff; but they were openly communicating for the first time. And suddenly, the thought of the Culture discussion didn't seem completely impossible. Ray's biggest problem, respect for authority, was not even insurmountable. After all, John realized, respect was a two-way street. By respecting Ray's input, he was showing respect for Ray's abilities and authority in his job. It wouldn't be so hard now to ask for Ray's respect in turn.

Stephanie nudged him. "Earth to John. Are you there?"

John laughed out loud. "Well, what are we waiting for? Let's light the candles."

No doubt about it, he had a lot of reasons to celebrate today.

Monday and Tuesday of the following week went by in a blur. Before he knew it, it was Tuesday night and John found himself at a pro basketball game, a night he had anticipated for weeks.

The crowd was on its feet. With just one minute left, the teams were tied and this free throw could determine the outcome. In the stands below their corporate box, men with bright blue painted faces and bodies waved and yelled frantically.

Whoosh. One basket.

Stephanie shouted something with her hands cupped around her mouth. Usually John shared her fervor, but he was distracted tonight by something his dad had said the last time they met: "Imagine a basketball game without a scoreboard and without a time clock. The game would soon lose purpose and deteriorate into chaos."

Tim had been talking about establishing visual work-flow controls that kept things moving along at a steady pace. He had given examples of how other service companies did it. An investment company, Star Team Investments, had used folders moving to different boxes to signal the movement of work from one stage to the next. But John was having a hard time coming up with a way to visually map how his team's work flowed. Software development was just . . . different, somehow.

"And it's in!" the announcer's voice bellowed from the speaker, bringing John's thoughts back to the game. Cheers erupted from the stands. The clock began to count down the final seconds.

On the floor, the play became frantic. One player fouled out. 3 . . . 2 . . . 1. . . . The final shot clanked off the side of the rim, and the buzzer sounded, signaling the game's end. The crowd poured onto the court. Their team was going to the playoffs.

They joined the crowds spilling out of the stadium and onto the streets. As they crossed the intersection, Stephanie asked about his plans for tomorrow's team meeting. John had taken his dad's advice to meet with the team away from the office and booked a meeting room in a resort in the low, rolling hills east of the city.

The idea of leaving the office had created a different mood within the group, an excitement and optimism that hadn't been there before. *Like we're embarking on a new adventure,* John had realized. And in a way, they were.

Just yesterday, Kiki had wrapped up the second-to-last revision on the existing code. Her production was increasing exponentially as each barrier to productivity was removed. *We're almost finished with the nonvalue-added work,* realized John. *And Blake will make sure we nail any new code the first time.*

As happy as John was with their progress, one look at the calendar had told him that they would need to move things up a notch to deliver the project by the drop-dead date. Tomorrow's meeting was critical; together, the team had to find a way to increase productivity by removing barriers. Walking by the fountain outside the stadium, he reached into his pocket for a penny and tossed it into the fountain.

"What's that for?" asked Stephanie.

"For luck," he said, and tossed in another for good measure.

The pennies worked. John's biggest worry—that Ray wouldn't be able to present the flowchart and guide the group through a discussion of how to remove the barriers—had proved unfounded. Ray had done a great job, and John felt his confidence in his team lead increase dramatically.

He hasn't had many opportunities to really function as a team lead before now, John realized. *Maybe that's why he's been so aggressive and jealous of authority.*

With this in mind, John pulled Ray aside after the meeting to address the next step in improving work flow.

"You know how I mentioned in the meeting that we'd have to increase the pace to meet our final deadline?" John began.

Ray nodded.

"Well, these suggestions for removing barriers that we came up with today will take us a long way toward that goal, but there's one more thing that's critical."

Ray looked interested.

"I'm hoping you would be willing to do some further evaluation for us. As a team, we need to know the rate at which work must flow to ensure we deliver on time," John explained. "You know how quickly we need to complete each unit of code. Here's a formula that will help," said John, handing a paper to Ray:

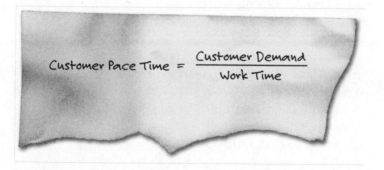

$$\text{Customer Pace Time} = \frac{\text{Customer Demand}}{\text{Work Time}}$$

Ray nodded. "I've seen something like this before. Years ago, when I worked at a manufacturing plant before I got my degree in software. That's how I hurt my back, at the plant," he said. "I can get this to you by Monday."

John felt like he was walking on air as he left the country club that night.

When John got into the office Monday morning, the light on his phone was blinking. He had a message. He pushed the button. It was Tracy from Mentec.

"I just wanted to put in a good word for Blake," she said. "It's been a night and day experience working with him. I just thought you should know."

John *did* know. Lately at work he had begun to feel like he was coming out of a long, dark tunnel into light so bright it made him squint.

His thoughts were interrupted by a soft knock on his open door. It was Todd.

"Hey, you ready to go?" he asked.

John motioned him into the room. "I just have to sign off on one thing," he said, locating a paper on his desk and scribbling out his signature. "I'll drop this by Mike's desk on the way out." He stood up. "All set. Let's go."

At the restaurant, over coffee, Todd handed over a crisp black binder with an elaborate flourish. "The training materials—well, just the first module, really, but it will give you an idea of where I'm going." Despite his best efforts to remain cool and detached, Todd's enthusiasm broke through.

"That training is the best thing I've done in years," he said.

Looking through the binder, John couldn't believe how much Todd had accomplished. It was just one week since John had enrolled him in a course on developing instructional design materials, and he was already producing results. Best of all, his work on the graphics hadn't suffered. If anything, it had improved.

The waitress arrived with their drinks and took their breakfast orders. Todd waited for her to leave and then said, "It's hard to explain. It's like I can see a light at the end of the tunnel for the first time in a long time, and it's not a train," he laughed.

John nodded; he suddenly had a strong sense of déjà vu.

On his way back to his office after the meeting with Todd, John stopped by Ray's office. It was probably too early to expect the calculation to be completed, but he thought he'd check in anyway.

As he entered the cube, Ray glanced up.

"Oh, I was just looking for you," he said. "I didn't find you in your office. Here you go," said Ray, handing him the calculations.

John scanned it eagerly. "I can't believe how quickly you pulled this together," he said.

"No sweat," said Ray. "I used to have to figure out how many motors had to be turned out in one day to meet our quota. This is just measuring something else using the same pace time calculation. I took the amount of code we have left to complete before the deadline, divided by the number of man hours we have left to do the work. In this case, we have four modules of code, each with five functions, making 20 total functions. And we have 200 man hours to complete it."

He pointed to a calculation on the sheet:

$$\frac{20 \text{ functions}}{200 \text{ man hours}} = .1 \text{ functions per man hour or } 1 \text{ function per } 10 \text{ man hours}$$

"It's an easy calculation once you have the data. It's getting the data that can take a little time," said Ray, modestly.

"Ray, this is a big deal," said John "I can't stress enough how this calculation changes everything. I thought we had plenty of time left, but we're going to have to bump things up a little for the next two weeks. We may have to work out some comp time after, or maybe I can pitch in a little."

Ray groaned and shook his head emphatically.

"No? Well, anyway, now we know exactly where we stand and we can make an educated decision of how to go forward. No more guessing. Now if we could just figure out a way to track the progress of code through this time frame. We need to be able to visually track where each unit is in the process."

"Magnets," said a voice from outside the cube.

John and Ray stared at each other for a moment, until Kiki came around the cube wall. She seemed a little embarrassed.

"I didn't mean to listen in; it's just so quiet with no one here yet. But, I was thinking, why not use magnets on the flow chart? Each magnet could represent a unit and we could post the flowchart on the magnetized whiteboard by your office. We can draw out all the critical steps within the flow and the deadlines, and then use color-coded magnets to identify each of us and where we are in our progress toward the target dates."

When no one said anything, Kiki instantly became apologetic.

"It's probably not what you were thinking," she said. "I just thought—"

"It's great. It's just what we need. Something simple to track our progress. Brilliant, Kiki, really!" said John.

The level of John's enthusiasm seemed to surprise both Kiki and Ray. But John had more than one reason to celebrate: This was the first time Kiki had openly offered a suggestion on anything—and it just happened to be the very answer he was looking for.

CHAPTER 6

Finally, a Structure that Puts Customers Where They Belong, at the Top

The Customer: The Real CEO

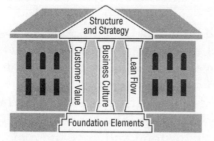

John's enthusiasm lasted through the weekend, but was severely dampened by the time he walked into the managers meeting on Monday morning. It wasn't the meeting itself that had him worried; it was what came afterward. John had asked to sit down with Kaye and Mike immediately following the meeting to discuss the Mentec training proposal, and John was dreading their reaction.

As the other managers left the room, John moved closer to Kaye and Mike who sat talking at the end of the table.

"Well, John, you asked to meet with us," said Kaye, as he sat down, "so I'll just let you guide the conversation." She sat back in her chair and folded her arms over her chest, in an exact replica of how Mike was sitting. It reminded him of how a judge might sit during a trial.

She just needs a robe—and maybe a stiff gray wig, thought John. Fortunately, the thought of Kaye in a judge's wig loosened John up enough to move forward.

Before the meeting, John had spent a lot of time thinking about how to approach the training subject. He had ultimately decided to spend much of his time outlining the changes in structure within his group that were driving results. In order for Kaye and Mike to embrace the proposal, they would need to at least understand a little about how this opportunity had come about—and why Mike's sales role had changed.

As John broached the idea, Mike's eyes widened.

"This is just what I was talking about!" stormed Mike to Kaye. "This falls completely within the realm of sales. This is a new product. We have vendors that have created training materials for us in the past. This isn't how we do things!" he ended, pushing back from the table as if to stand and leave the room.

"Now, Mike, just a moment," said Kaye, motioning for him to stop. "John, I can see how lucrative this training idea can be for us. But I agree with Mike that you're not fully utilizing the resources around you. Why don't you consider using the vendors we've used before to create the training? And Mike should be involved in creating a sales presentation on this training product, since I'm sure Mentec will put it out for bid and—"

"No, they're not putting it out for bid," said John, trying to rein in his own frustration. "We didn't ask Mike's group to create a sales presentation simply because we don't need one. In our daily discussions, Mentec asked us to develop this training. Based on our recent performance, they trust us to deliver. We listen to them. They know we understand their unique needs."

"Are you suggesting sales didn't?" Mike asked loudly.

"I'm just saying we're not competing with anyone else," said John in a low but serious voice. "We've got the deal already. And with Todd creating the training, instead of an outside vendor, we're able to provide this product at no additional cost to AXD. That's the best possible world for us, right? To find a revenue stream that doesn't cost us anything to provide?"

John looked over at Kaye as he said this. Her eyes narrowed, and she studied him in silence for a moment. John could tell she was torn between the undeniable fiscal reality of what he had just said and her reservations about his unconventional approach.

"Let's take a break," said Kaye, holding up a finger to silence Mike, who had just opened his mouth to begin a fresh tirade. Mike threw up his arms in disgust. "No," she continued. "We're going to table this discussion and cool down and review this proposal in one week. I'm out of town for the next few days. We'll meet next Tuesday. I'll have my assistant schedule the time with both of you."

She stood, signaling the end of the discussion. In response, Mike began to flip aggressively through the pages of the proposal, exclaiming in anger at different sections. John hardly noticed. He was picturing himself sitting in the traffic jam, waiting for the blockage to clear. He felt the same helplessness now as he had then; there was nothing he could do. After sitting for a moment, John thanked them for their time and left the room.

John's frustration over the meeting with Kaye and Mike lingered like a migraine during the rest of the week, dampening his enthusiasm and clouding his vision. Fortunately, his team didn't seem to perceive the change in his mood and continued to move forward with energy and enthusiasm.

On Friday, John was standing in line at the dry cleaners when he recognized the familiar face of Jay Jackson from Trenneth. Remembering their warm reunion at the Thai Café, John stepped forward to clap Jay on the shoulder.

"Oh, hey, John, how are you doing?" Jay turned from the counter and clenched John's hand in a firm handshake. "My wife gave up ironing shirts years ago," he said, motioning to the pile of laundry the woman behind the counter was carrying away. "By the way, I wanted to tell you, I ran into your boss, Kaye Gines, on the red-eye last night. She had a lot of questions about the training proposal for Mentec. Sounds like you're shaking things up over there at AXD."

Jay glanced at the line of customers behind them and motioned for John to follow him.

"I've known Kaye a long time. We go way back. I'll tell you one thing, she's always been the cautious type—overly cautious in my opinion—but she's also got a good head. She'll come around. Don't give up. You're on the right track."

Smiling, Jay pushed open the door and waved a goodbye. John wasn't sure how long he stood there before he realized the store was empty. He tried to ignore the strange look the counter attendant gave him as he approached the counter and handed over his shirts.

"Long day," he said in explanation. She didn't reply, which was really nothing new, John realized.

I can't wait to talk to Dad, he thought as he left the store. He was missing the constant dialogue and direction, but he didn't want to intrude on his dad's time with his team. *When Dad gets back, he'll have something to say about all of this, some way to keep moving forward.*

Thinking of his dad, John suddenly realized something he'd never thought of before: His dad had gone through all of what John was going through now, but without a mentor. All the frustration. All the worries. All the insecurities. He'd done it without someone to call.

No wonder it means so much for him to talk about it with me, he thought. *He had to learn much of this through trial and error, figure it all out himself, with no one to guide him. Could I have done that?*

The question stopped John cold. He quickly decided to follow Kaye's lead and table that discussion until later.

Early Monday morning, John picked up his home phone on the fourth ring and heard his dad's familiar voice. Tim sounded rejuvenated. "Meet me on the roof of your building in one hour," Tim said. "I've got something to show you."

"On top of my building? Are you here in town?" asked John, confused.

"Your mom and I got in late last night and stayed in the city at the Hilton," he said. "Don't ask questions, just be there in an hour."

John arrived early, but his dad was already there, standing at the east side of the building, looking out over the city. John had never been up here, but there were signs that other people had, including some candles and discarded takeout containers.

As he approached, his dad sat down in an old metal folding chair, which instantly collapsed beneath him.

John rushed forward to help him up, but his dad waved him off, laughing.

"I'm fine, just fine" he said, standing and brushing the loose gravel from the roof off his clothes. He studied the pile of metal momentarily. "It looked all right, but it really wasn't built to do the job. Hmmm. Sounds a lot like AXD." A couple months back, a comment like that would have bothered John. But things had changed dramatically since then, and he could see his dad's point.

"By the way, how'd you like Stephanie's present?" Tim asked, turning to look at the city again. "She thought she'd replace that artifact you've been carrying around."

"It's great, but it doesn't really replace it," said John, pulling the paper out of his pocket and waving it in the air. "This is portable. But I've been wondering about what this all means," he said, pointing to where he'd filled in the roof. "I have a lot of questions for you."

Tim smiled. "I thought you would. I brought you up here to the roof to talk about that." Tim looked out over the city. "You know, it's nice being on top. Being on top usually means you are the most important, the one with the pull, the one who sets the standards."

Tim pulled an organizational chart out of his pocket. John thought it looked familiar, like the one out of his textbooks. *By the way, where had his textbooks gone?* He couldn't remember seeing them for ages.

"In most organizations, the CEO is at the top of the organizational chart; but not in a Value-Centered Enterprise. Look, here's the organizational chart for my team," Tim pulled another paper from his pocket. The breeze lifted it in the air, and for a moment, Tim struggled to straighten it out for John to get a good look. "See, I'm at the bottom and the customer is at the top.

"Now, that's backward and upside down from how most businesses are organized, but a Value-Centered Enterprise is never afraid to look at business differently and buck conventional wisdom."

He pulled the paper straight again, and they examined it. "This shows customers where they stand."

John felt the questions welling up in him. "But how did you get to the point where everyone buys into this? Didn't leadership or sales resist it?"

"They still do," Tim said, smiling empathetically. "It's a slow transition. Notice I didn't show you an organizational chart for the whole airline; a lot of my company is still mired in tradition. But our team gets results, so I've been given a lot of leeway."

As Tim mentioned this, John could sense a decrease in his father's energy and enthusiasm. Tim kicked at the gravel beneath his feet. "It's funny when you think about it, because most companies make a big deal about working together, but then they employ a traditional structure that prevents it from truly happening. Dividing organizations into departments actually impedes work flow and builds organizational territories."

Dividing organizations into departments actually impedes work flow and builds organizational territories.

"You see, most companies group people into departments, which teaches us to *depart* from one another. Or they group team members into divisions, which teaches us to *divide* instead of unify."

Down below, in a school yard, the two of them watched as two girls' soccer teams, one dressed in blue and the other in red, struggled against each other to score a goal. John was reminded of the basketball game the other night. The competition. The winners and the losers.

Almost like he was talking to himself, Tim continued, "Traditional businesses can't be truly value centered because the departments within them are all seeking to prove their own worth while ignoring the importance of working together with other counterparts to properly serve the customer.

"But, you know," said Tim, turning to John, as if he had just remembered he was there, "a determined leader can create a Value-Centered Enterprise anywhere—within a manufacturing or service industry, or even within a company that hasn't fully embraced the philosophy. Just look at me . . . and you." The thought seemed to cheer Tim.

"Here, let's find a spot to sit down that won't break under my ample girth. This is really what I wanted to show you."

John and Tim found a cement ledge surrounding the air-conditioning equipment and sat down. Tim turned over his organizational chart on his knee and labeled it Traditional Business Structure. Then he began to draw boxes all over the sheet, giving them different department names, including marketing, accounting, customer service, and so on. It all looked very familiar.

"This is how a traditional business is set up. Each department is stuck in its own box and focuses on its own expertise, and each department is seeking to prove its own worth," he told John.

Tim was interrupted as the air-conditioning units turned on, creating a deafening roar.

"Why don't we go down to my apartment, and I'll fry you an egg before I leave for work?" yelled John into his dad's ear. Tim nodded and they headed for the door.

"Your mom is sleeping in," he yelled back.

On their way down the hall, they ran into John's neighbor, an eccentric artist, who always had bright paint underneath her nails and matching head scarves in wild, vibrant colors. "How's it going today, Judy?" John asked.

"Not so good, not so good," she said, in a scratchy voice. "This building is nice, but try to get them to fix your dripping faucet, just try that," she said, sighing.

Tim nodded sympathetically as she turned into her apartment and waved goodbye. He and Tim paused before John's door.

"You know," Tim said. "What she said sounds so familiar. It's like I said: The traditional business structure looks okay from the outside. But get inside, and you realize it's broken and almost impossible to fix. Most executives just aren't willing or able to take it on. Gradually, they become acclimated to the problems and expect complaints, poor service, inconsistency, and negative customer experiences as a normal part of doing business. Sort of like putting a frog in cold water versus boiling; they don't give it a second thought."

He slapped John on the back and headed down the hallway.

At AXD that morning, John met with Ray. John had decided to put him in charge of developing coding standards for the group, which he would love—but with one catch.

"I'd like you to lead the group in developing these standards," said John. "In a sense, you'll be the facilitator. I'll leave it up to you to set the meeting schedule, but I'd appreciate an invite."

The eager look in Ray's eyes told John what he already knew: This was right up Ray's alley, and John hoped the interaction with the group would help Ray to function more as part of the team.

"On another note, Ray," continued John, "I wanted to thank you for the bang-up job you did on the Value Stream diagram. You've saved our group a lot of headaches and the company a lot of money. When you get back to your desk, I want you to take a look at the e-mail I sent Kaye about your recent contributions. I cc'd you."

Ray appeared flabbergasted. "Here's a small token of my appreciation," said John, handing Ray a large red envelope. In it was a gift certificate for a series of visits to a message therapist. "You mentioned that you were thinking of going to one to see if it helped your back. How's that chair, anyway? Is it helping?"

Ray swallowed hard. *Was he struggling with emotion?* John wondered.

"The chair is great," was all Ray said, but John could see that he appreciated the gesture.

John hesitated. What he had to do next was difficult. In the moment's silence, Ray looked around the room and began to rise. "I better get back to my cube. . . ."

"Um, hold on would you?" John realized his voice was a littler louder than he had intended. Ray sat back down and looked at him curiously. "I just have one more thing before you go. It has to do with some other standards . . . for the way we interact as a team and our attitudes at work. It's seven commitments, actually. It will just take a minute."

Ray nodded and pulled his chair in closer. And before John knew it, he and Ray were having their first conversation about attitude control.

John took Stephanie to dinner that night at the Thai Café. Stephanie was in a cheerful mood. She'd had her hair done at her favorite place, Jovance, and was wearing a new summer dress from Stalaro's Boutique. No one was having a crisis, but they hadn't been to the Café in a while, and he missed the place.

The owner, Niran, was seating guests that night, and he welcomed the pair as old friends. "It's been a long time," he said, as he handed them their menus.

"Too long," agreed John, watching the busy activity behind Niran. The restaurant was a family affair. He knew that Niran's oldest daughter did the bookkeeping, while his only son managed the place. The recipes had come from Niran's wife, who had been the original cook. These days, she ordered the supplies and interacted with vendors. It was a small operation and they kept it simple—and it worked well.

Looking around, John remembered the last thing his dad had told him that morning: "In Value-Centered Management, it's important to keep things simple. I've seen small businesses with 100 workers who had an accounting department with a dozen people because they let things get too complicated. Be careful to limit the activities of your teams to only those that deliver value to the customer."

John realized he had been staring at the menu for more than five minutes without talking. He looked up at Stephanie, who smiled. "Thinking of trying something new tonight?" she asked. As she said it, he realized that was a good idea.

"I think so. For starters, I think I'll try the Tom Kah," he said, as another of Niran's daughters approached their table. "I'm in the mood for something new."

John stayed up late into the night looking over the diagram his dad had drawn up during breakfast. It mapped out the structure of a Value-Centered Business. On it, one large Value Stream full of several Direct Service Teams was supported by seven Indirect Service Teams.

Around the edges of the paper and overflowing onto the back of the page, Tim had scrawled notes outlining the purpose of each Indirect Service Team. John turned the paper in his hands, reviewing his dad's words:

Value management

- Continually identifies and maintains what the customer values and ensures those values are being properly incorporated into all service teams within the company.
- Keeps current through value focus groups.

Planning and analysis

- Coordinates and fulfills planning and analysis necessary for short- and long-term success.
- Key planning areas:
  - Business strategy
  - Forecasting and budgeting
  - Financial analysis
  - Tax preparation
  - Market research

Accounting

- Accounts for the money coming into and going out of the organization on a day-to-day basis.
- Limits activities to only what is absolutely necessary to supply the type of business it serves, which may include:
  - Ensuring money gets to the bank.
  - Accounting for and pursuing money customers owe the company.
  - Ensuring team members are paid in a timely manner.
  - Accurately inputting data into the accounting systems so the planning team can access this information for more detailed analysis and reporting.

Partnership management

- Selects the right vendors and support organizations to build long-term mutually beneficial relationships and deliver value to the customer.
- Keeps inventories low by negotiating agreements that supply quality products and services at the point of need.
- Communicates positive and/or negative performance information.

Human resources

- Helps team members enter the organization in a professional manner.
- Establishes development systems to allow for team member growth.
- Develops user-friendly forms.
- Protects the organization by ensuring all activities are carried out according to employee law.
- Assists in the development of compensation and performance management systems.
- Helps team members exit the organization in a professional manner.

Information technology

- Manages the company's ability to move, locate, and store the information necessary to consistently create and deliver value.
- Purchases equipment and software based on what's needed, not what's popular.
- Minimizes equipment while maximizing information flow.
- Focuses on having the right software and equipment, not the best.
- Understands that solving the problem correctly is more important than resolving it quickly.

Kaizen

- Manages cultural improvement systems throughout the company.
- Assists direct and indirect service teams in implementing value-centered solutions.
- Promotes and trains team members in systematic improvement using standard tools.

Putting the paper down, John remembered his dad's last instruction. Tim had been very clear that the Direct Service Team is responsible for delivering products and services to the customer, while the Indirect Service Teams provide support to the Direct Service Team.

"That's a key point," Tim had said, his pen retracing the arrows between the teams. "Direct Service Teams only utilize the Indirect Service Teams *as necessary* for a specific business function; each Service Team—direct and indirect—is focused on best meeting the customers' needs. A weekly Value-Stream Performance meeting of all the key team members and leaders of the Value Stream to discuss the organizational performance based on the 3S Health Card makes sure everyone is on the same page and things are getting done. I'll tell you more about the 3S Health Card later.

"The key to all this," Tim had said finally, circling the diagram, "is that instead of establishing departmental kingdoms, we must establish service teams that support and operate the Value Stream."

Here he had leaned toward John and said with significance, "Once you've done that, you'll find you have fewer complaints, improved customer service, increased morale, less quality problems, and consistent delivery of value to the customer. And better work flow, of course." To emphasize his point, he had drawn a large exclamation point on the page.

John had been transfixed. Wasn't this they type of relationship he had been trying to outline to Kaye and Mike the other day, with miserable results? *Of course they needed sales,* John thought, setting down his fork. *But in a different way. They needed sales to support them, as needed.* It made so much sense to John, it was as if he had already come to understand this concept on his own, and his dad was just filling in the blanks.

The morning's meeting with Kaye and Mike was set for eleven, so John was shocked to find Kaye waiting for him in his office when he arrived at seven-thirty on Tuesday. She stood up from the chair she was sitting in as he walked in and shook his hand. *How long has she been waiting here?* John wondered.

"I'm sorry," she said, "but I need to talk to you in private. I want you to tell me more about your approach without upsetting Mike."

John sat down in the chair next to hers and took a look at her face. She looked tired, with faint dark circles under her eyes.

"I've been thinking about your concepts involving this Value-Centered Management. I think I'm ready to listen, given the results you're pulling in."

Eager to explain, John quickly summarized the main point of what he'd learned so far from his dad: Everything within a Value-Centered Enterprise focuses on delivering what the customer values. He drew a diagram with the customer on top:

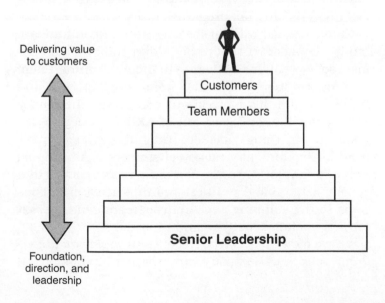

Delivering value to customers

Customers

Team Members

Senior Leadership

Foundation, direction, and leadership

Kaye studied the diagram thoughtfully, but said nothing. Thanking his lucky stars for his dad, John pulled out the Value-Centered Business diagram Tim had drawn up.

"You see," he said, "within a Value-Centered Enterprise, Direct Service Teams like my department only utilize the Indirect Service Teams, like marketing or sales, *as necessary* for specific business functions. That's why I didn't involve Mike in the meetings with Mentec."

In explanation, John handed Kaye the pages he had put together outlining the purposes of the seven different Indirect Service Teams. She began to go through each one, slowly, with John pointing out things along the way.

"You see, the Planning and Analysis Service Team, for example, ensures AXD is prepared for short-term and long-term success," explained John. "It's different from Accounting, which meets day-to-day financial commitments. The Planning and Analysis team's main responsibility is to provide key planning in the forms of: business strategy, forecasting and budget, financial analysis, and tax preparation."

Kaye nodded without looking up and continued to study the paper in front of her. John couldn't read her face, so he went on, motioning to the Accounting Team.

"Accounting is separate from the Planning and Analysis team. It's more about controlling the money that comes into and goes out of AXD on a day-to-day basis, doing things like ensuring the money is received, accounting for money customers owe and pursuing it, making sure the company pays vendors in a timely fashion, and putting data into accounting systems so the Planning and Analysis team can access it for more detailed analysis and reporting."

Kaye didn't react. *Why wasn't she saying anything?* John wondered. He wasn't sure whether he should continue. He knew he was about to address a touchy subject at AXD. The incredible size of the accounting department at AXD had always been a mystery to him.

"The main problem with this group, usually," said John. "Is that it tends to get too big—in scope and staffing. Accounting should only do what is absolutely necessary to support the type of business it serves."

Kaye laughed. John thought it sounded like an acknowledgement of the problem, but he was unsure. When Kaye still didn't look up, he went on.

"Internal IT can have some problems maintaining focus, too," said John, skipping down the page a bit. "It's easy for them to get caught up in the newest and greatest. But it's more important to have the right software and equipment to meet our needs so we can serve clients. They're two different things: The newest software isn't always the right software. Also, rather than focusing on getting through the service tickets as quickly as they can, they should concentrate on resolving problems correctly. That involves changing the whole value structure in the group because, right now, the emphasis is on speed and volume versus fixing core issues by removing the root causes of problems."

Again, Kaye laughed, and John felt an overwhelming surge of self-consciousness. *He was really going out on a limb here,* he realized. *Was she laughing at him?*

"You can see for yourself what the roles of the other departments are," he said, lamely. "Most of the teams you'll recognize. The Kaizen team is new, though. Kaizen means a change for the better. I can go into it a little more if you'd like . . ." His words trailed off at the end.

John waited for what seemed like hours before Kaye finished reviewing the paper and looked up, studying him. Finally, she spoke.

"So you're proposing we reorganize the entire division?"

It was an honest question, empty of sarcasm or anger; and John felt relieved. Still, he thought for a moment before replying.

"I'm not expecting that to happen now or even in the near future," he said, choosing his words carefully. "But I'd like the ability to interact with sales and the other departments a little differently. I need to be able to draw on their resources, as needed. I need to be able to count on them to help me best meet customer needs, even in unconventional ways."

Kaye sat back and eyed him, considering.

"That doesn't seem unreasonable," she said finally, nodding. "Maybe we can explore some of these ideas as a project. I can see where you're coming from now; and the results you're pulling in certainly make a strong case for some flexibility. But Mike's an important player in our company, and this is going to be a hard sell for him."

John nodded. *That's an understatement*, he thought.

Kaye opened the lid of the coffee she had left untouched throughout their meeting. She took a sip and eyed John seriously.

"Remember when I told you we didn't need a maverick?" she asked, raising an eyebrow. As she said it, John felt his stomach lurch. *Was this where she lowered the boom?* Kaye just smiled. "Well, I'm beginning to think that maybe, just maybe, I was wrong."

CHAPTER 7

From a Traditional Organization to a Value-Centered Organization: Now, How Do You Stay Healthy?

Measurement: Maintaining Value, Culture, and Flow

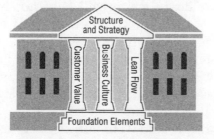

When Mike walked into Kaye's office for their meeting later that morning, John was surprised at the hot flash of anger he felt. They both greeted each other politely, then busied themselves with paperwork, so they wouldn't have to talk.

As Kaye entered the room, John leaned forward in his chair, as if preparing to pounce, and some advice from his dad ran through his mind.

"You know how kids fight," Tim had warned. "They're mad one moment and the next they're best friends again and out playing basketball together. They have this innate ability to bounce back from conflict. We need to develop the same ability at the office so we can have a knock-down-drag-out conflict in the boardroom one day and the next, be able to work together again, free of hostility and resentment. Leaders have to demonstrate that skill if they want team members to adopt it."

John rolled his shoulders and stretched a little as he mentally readjusted his attitude. He was determined to control his attitude.

Fortunately, Mike seemed to have come to the table in the same conciliatory state of mind and, with Kaye somewhat behind John, the meeting went better than expected. Of course, Mike wasn't happy, but, after a short discussion, he accepted the idea of Todd creating the training materials instead of an outside vendor.

"If he can do it then, great," Mike finally said, a little stiffly. "I just hope this doesn't turn around and bite us with a shoddy product."

In response, John slid copies of the first training module developed by Todd across the glass and steel table to Kaye and Mike. After a brief review, Mike's concern seemed to abate.

"Not bad," he said. "I'm surprised. Can I hold onto this?" he asked, sliding it into his briefcase.

"Just let me know if you need anything," said Mike. "We'd be glad to help out."

Kaye and John looked at each other and smiled. That was exactly what John had hoped to hear.

On the way back to his office, John began to whistle, but the second verse of "Zippity Doo Dah" was interrupted as he rounded the corner to his office and ran into Blake.

"How's it going?" he asked, slapping Blake on the back in a congratulatory way. John felt on top of the world. Everything was going so much better than he ever expected.

Blake didn't say anything. But the look on his face answered John's question: Things were not going well.

"I need some advice," said Blake with a concerned expression. John nodded and led the way into his office.

"I'm having a problem with some of the new code," said Blake. "Well, really, just one specific piece." Blake corrected himself. "There's one feature that Ray absolutely insists on building differently than Mentec outlined.

"I know he thinks he's doing Mentec a favor in the long run—the way they want it done is so limited and they'll outgrow it quickly; but his way is more complicated than Mentec can handle right now. They're not going to like it; and I know you don't want us to have to do rewrites."

"Well, right, because when we redo work, we're not making money, we're burning it," John said.

As he spoke, John realized his tone was sharper than he had intended. *This isn't Blake's fault,* he reminded himself. *I really haven't clarified his role with the team. This is my fault.*

"Okay," said John, leaning forward in his chair toward Blake. "This is what we'll do: Schedule a meeting for tomorrow morning. Get the whole team together." Blake nodded and got up to leave. "And Blake," added

John. "Let's meet at four o'clock this afternoon. I'll have some more direction for you by then," he said.

Blake nodded, looking relieved.

Good, John thought. *He's keeping an eye on the things the customer values. We've just got to give him a way to communicate that knowledge with the team with some authority.*

John knew there was a communication issue arising in his team—how to solve this one? He remembered some of his business textbooks. He hadn't looked at them forever. *Maybe I could find something there,* thought John. He stood and headed for the door. He would grab his favorite leadership book and bring it back here to look through. His mind raced through the day's schedule. It was busy, but he would find the time.

John's phone rang at two, while he was eating a late lunch at his desk, his book open wide in front of him. "Dad!" he said. Tim chuckled at John's evident enthusiasm.

"What great timing. I'm struggling with a leadership challenge right now," said John, stumbling over his words. "I've been looking in an old management textbook for a solution to a problem that came up today, and I'm realizing again how many things I'm not doing that it says I should be doing."

John felt the old familiar panic coming back.

"Whoa, slow down," Tim said. "The thing to remember with all of business education—and the reason I worry about you spending so much time in those books—is that too many leaders think they have to do everything the way it's outlined there, even if they don't need it."

"So, you're saying all the time I spent in college is useless? I mean, I know you didn't go to school, and you're doing great, but—"

Tim held up his hand to stop John.

"That's not what I'm saying at all. Actually, just the opposite. Value-Centered Management makes your textbook knowledge more effective because it teaches you how to put that knowledge to work for you—as valuable tools—instead of you working for the books.

"Without Value-Centered Management, leaders end up implementing process and systems that are superfluous. They don't need them; but they do them because they think they should. That's why you'll see a company that turns a couple million dollars a year with a huge finance department of 25 people. That company is overdoing things, running reports and keeping records that they'll never use, all because they read it somewhere or someone told them they should.

"For companies that have a product customers really want, it's possible to be wasteful and still turn a profit. So, they never stop to consider how much money they throw away on unproductive activities. Do you hear what I'm saying?"

John took a deep breath. "Maybe," he said.

"Look," said Tim, "the most important thing to remember about management education is that you only use the tools that your company needs. If you only need one accounting person to pay the bills and collect the bills, then you keep it simple, and you only have one person. Organizational structure must be based on the diverse Value Streams that exist within the company. Don't make things more complicated than they have to be."

As his dad spoke, John felt his mind clearing. *He's right*, John thought. *I need to focus on doing what is needed, not on doing everything that was ever written.*

Focus on doing what is needed, not on doing everything that was ever written.

John closed the book and pushed it aside. He stood up and began to pace his office as he explained the conversation with Blake.

"It just seems like I haven't given him the right communication process or authority to control the value flow within the group," said John. "Any advice?"

"Sure," said Tim. "You know, this is the next part of the roof: Maintaining the Culture. And it goes hand-in-hand with Measurement and Control and Cultural Improvement."

John picked up the small figurine Stephanie had given him and studied the writing within the roof. The fluorescent light glinted off it sharply.

"You've made some great progress with Ray and the rest of the team. But remember, no matter how hard you work to arrive at the right culture, you must work even harder to maintain it," said Tim. "Never assume because you had a good meeting or made a great speech that your positive team dynamics will be maintained. You have to create an environment in the workplace that reminds team members of their commitments to customer value and to each other. You have to create and maintain a successful culture.

"The best way to do this is by example. You have to demonstrate an absolute commitment to customer value," Tim said. In the background, John could hear the screen door slam and the porch swing creak. He could picture his father sitting there, looking out over the water as he spoke.

"It also helps to post visuals throughout the workplace. At my place, we post the Seven Commitments and KIND—and we make a point to talk about them a lot. Every morning, we review our values during a morning stretch. Then, on Friday, we get together and read one of the seven commitments and discuss it more in depth. It works for us, but you decide what your group needs.

"Of course, even with the postings," he continued, "you'll run into trouble sometimes. Some team members, like Ray, will have a hard time accepting parts of the culture and living it consistently. You have to deal with that right away and straight on, because—as you know from firsthand experience—although it takes a lot of effort to build a culture, it takes very little effort to tear it down.

"In a Value-Centered Enterprise, honest communication is critical. How often do you have performance reviews at AXD?" asked Tim.

"At the end of the year, for sure; some managers do them twice a year," said John.

"Well, everyone in your organization should have feedback about their performance at least twice a year, and it should be honest feedback. And, everyone who deserves a top rating should get it and the financial rewards that come with it. It's de-motivating for employees to go into a performance review knowing that their boss has been instructed to severely limit the number of superior ratings. If an employee is doing great, tell them and reward them. If they're not up to snuff, tell them."

"No manager likes to hurt their employees' feelings," said John, hesitantly.

"You don't do it in a hurtful way. But one of the most common reasons things don't get done in corporate America is because leaders don't tell it like it is. So, you'll have a team member who has wasted years working at far below his capacity, simply because no one has ever had the guts to tell him the hard truth. Meanwhile, the employee feels frustrated because he's being held back professionally and doesn't understand why. He's a dead man walking. Our team members need the truth to become better people and professionals.

"And the knife cuts both ways, too. Many organizations don't go as far as they could because team members don't feel they can honestly express what they see," said Tim.

"So, what should I do? What should I say?" John asked. "I've got a meeting late this afternoon with Blake and tomorrow with the team . . ."

"This is where measurement and control comes in," said Tim. "When you're addressing problems with the culture, you need to have data that identifies and validates the problem areas. It's hard to argue with data," said Tim, "and I know just where you should start.

"Go check your fax, I just sent something over," Tim said. As John walked out to the fax machine, Tim continued.

Value Points	Service Teams	VS Processes	Challenges	Kaizen
Speed	Related service team(s)	Specifics	Specifics	Specifics
Quality	Related service team(s)	Specifics	Specifics	Specifics
Communication	Related service team(s)	Specifics	Specifics	Specifics

"This chart is developed from information you collect during meetings with your Value-Management Service Team," said Tim. "You should be holding these meetings regularly, on a schedule. And at every meeting, Blake should redetermine what the group values, or what I call the Value Points. That's the first column," said Tim.

"One of the biggest mistakes companies make is assuming that the needs of their customers remain the same—that they never change—when really a customer's priorities are in constant flux. Right now, Mentec values simplicity, and they want training. But as they become more comfortable with the software, as Ray says, they may begin to want more functionality. You have to keep your finger on their pulse.

"Look at the second column. Once Blake has determined the needs of the customer, maybe on a

monthly basis, then he identifies which team or team
member is responsible for providing that value point.
Once we know that, we look more closely at that person on the team to determine which of their processes
impact that Value Point and what challenges they face
that might prevent the Value Point from being ful-
filled. Kaizen is the last column. It's where we identify
the improvements that need to take place; how people
or teams are going to change to meet the identified
Value Points."

"So, Blake puts this all together himself?" asked
John.

"No, and that's important," said Tim. "It's his job
to identify the Value Points and the teams that provide
those Value Points, but, from there on, he needs the
input from team members to identify processes, challenges, and Kaizen improvements."

Outside his office, John watched as Kiki shyly approached Ray and spoke to him. Their conversation
was brief, and Kiki seemed to cower a little during
Ray's response.

"My group sometimes has a hard time working together on the simplest things," John said in a low
voice as he turned back to his office. "I can't imagine
them brainstorming improvements together on a regular basis."

"That's because they haven't had much experience
working together as a unified team. They've just been
four individuals doing their own individual jobs.
They've never really had to pull together before. You'll
see. It might be rough at first, but as your team
spends more time hammering things out, they'll get
better at it, and you'll see greater unity."

John wasn't so sure. How would Kiki muster the
courage to vocalize her thoughts with the group? And
if she did, how would the team respond? A picture of

Ray sitting silent and brooding flashed in his mind. He sighed.

"I know," said Tim. "It's hard to see how it could possibly happen. But it can. Not at first, maybe, but with practice. You've got this meeting tonight with Blake, then tomorrow with the group. Give it a try. It'll work. You'll see.

"And remember, your job is to facilitate this experience and create an environment that is inclusive and based on RESPECT."

"Like the song?" asked John, confused.

"No, RESPECT is an acronym that outlines how you create a professional, productive environment in the workplace. Here, let me shoot it over to you."

In a moment, a box popped up, indicating John had an e-mail. He opened it and read:

RESPECT

Rewarding place to work

Empathetic to our customers

Strive to be better in every aspect through Kaizen

Professional, we live by high ethical standards

Everyone is involved, no barriers

Client focused, as our client succeed, we succeed

Teamwork is the key to our success

"So, I just—"   Just then a loud noise outside John's door interrupted their conversation.

"I'll give it a try."

As he hung up, two young, burly guys appeared in his doorway.

"We've got a desk. Where does it go?" one asked.

John was surprised. He hadn't ordered a new desk, and Kaye hadn't mentioned anything about one, but he had to admit it was needed. The desk he'd inherited from Cheryl had two broken drawers and was chipped and scarred.

"Put it right in here," he said, smiling. The desk looked nice. He stepped out of the way into the hallway as the men began to push and shove and tilt the desk through his door frame.

"Will it fit?" John asked, concerned.

"Yeah, it'll fit," one of the men said, giving the desk a fierce yank.

In the end it really *didn't* fit, and the desk had to be hauled away, leaving John more dissatisfied with his old desk than he had been before. Every chip seemed exaggerated.

The phone rang. John picked it up, fingering a chip on the desk. He immediately recognized the cheery voice of Kaye's assistant.

"John, I'm so sorry about the desk. No one thought to measure the doorway; we just assumed it would work. You have that funny column in the hallway just outside your office, too, which makes things difficult. Oh, well, we'll reassess things and get another desk out your way soon. Sorry for the inconvenience."

John assured her it was all right and looked up at the clock. The desk saga, as he had labeled it, had taken over an hour; and he had been barred from his office for the entire time. He had just enough time to get the chart ready for his meeting with Blake.

By the time Blake arrived, John had recovered from his desk disappointment. And, as usual, his dad turned out to be right. When John presented the Customer Value Alignment Chart, Blake was thrilled.

"This will be a great way to introduce the discussion of the new module tomorrow," said Blake, taking a blank copy of the chart that John had created for him. "I don't know how you come up with these things. But I'm glad you do."

John felt a little sheepish; after all, he wasn't the one who had come up with it. But he decided that, in this case, what Blake didn't know wouldn't hurt him.

The next day, John turned the last half of the team meeting over to Blake, who passed out a chart with the first two columns completed. John watched the group's faces intently. They looked surprised at first, then a little skeptical.

But Blake didn't seem to notice, leading the group enthusiastically through the exercise. John was impressed with Blake's approach. When Blake reached the second value point, labeled Simplicity, he guided the team through identifying the absolute minimum functionality needed to complete the next module.

The approach wasn't confrontational, and after raising a few mild objections, even Ray agreed to keep things within the basic specs. John wouldn't have believed it if he hadn't seen it with his own eyes.

When he got home later that night, John called Tim to report his success.

"So, Kiki didn't say anything during the whole meeting, which was a little discouraging," said John. "But she was supportive of the group's Kaizen improvements and so was Todd. Ray brought up a few concerns, but with the value of Simplicity guiding the discussion, it was hard for him to argue for the added functionality. It was amazing how having the value points in front of us clarified our direction forward."

"Give Kiki time to gain more confidence; she'll come around. But looking at the results from today, it makes you wonder why more leaders don't take this approach, doesn't it?" his father asked.

"There are a couple more tools for measurement and control that I want you to see. They're a little different; they help you to see the flow of the Value Stream as a whole, instead of within isolated areas. They make sure you can see the whole forest, not just the trees.

"So many companies miss that. Have you ever noticed that sometimes a company institutes an improvement that starts off with a bang, by dramatically increasing revenue or cutting costs, but it isn't sustainable, and in the end, overall, it actually drives revenue down or costs up? I've got a couple of charts that provide a uniform, consistent way of determining the overall health of your group, so you can gauge whether an improvement is really working and how your organization is doing from week to week."

John thought of the new desk, which would have been a huge improvement for his office. He looked at the papers, binders, and boxes stacked against the wall in his office. What he wouldn't give for working drawers. If only someone had bothered to measure the door. His thoughts were interrupted as his dad went on.

"Remember, you should always focus on what the Value Stream is doing as a whole because that gives you the true condition of the organization. I'll fax the two charts over in the morning. Take a look at them, and we can talk some time tomorrow."

John opened his mouth to reply, but his father had already hung up. John laughed at the irony of it: The last few weeks had been filled with change; but some things never did.

The charts John pulled off the fax in the morning were intimidating, and John had to fight the urge to put them aside. The first was labeled 3S Health Card:

VALUE-CENTERED ENTERPRISE, INC.
3S HEALTH CARD

Categories	Measurements	Weekly Target	01/07 Week 1	01/14 Week 2	01/21 Week 3	01/28 Week 4	02/01 Week 5	Monthly Total	Monthly Target	Off Target?
STATE OF THE CUSTOMER	Value rating (%)	100%	95%	99%	98%	91%	95%	96%	100%	-4%
	No. of complaints	0	1	1	0	0	1	3	0	(3)
	No. of leads	5	10	8	4	11	6	8	5	
	No. of customers served	50	39	45	42	56	67	249	200	(49)
	No. of 1st-time customers	5	0	1	3	0	0	1	5	(4)
STATE OF THE VALUE STREAM	No. of implemented kaizens	10	2	3	1	5	6	17	5	
	No. of team members	10.0	10.0	10.0	10.0	10.0	10.0	10	10.0	
	Revenue per team member	$1,000	$1,000	$1,000	$1,000	$1,000	$1,000	$1,000	$1,000	
	No. of problem files	5.0	1.0	1.0	1.0	1.0	1.0	5	25.0	(20.0)
	Average point-to-point time	35	24	34	45	23	45	34	35	
STATE OF THE COMPANY	Revenue—sales growth	$2,000	$2,000	$2,000	$2,000	$2,000	$2,000	$10,000	$10,000	
	Bank account credits (+)		$2,000	$2,500	$2,300	$2,200	$2,100	$11,100		
	Bank account debits (–)		$1,500	$1,575	$1,000	$542	$237	$4,864		
	Value stream net cash deposites to bank	$500	$500	$925	$1,300	$1,658	$1,863	$6,246	$2,000	
	Week ending cash balance (Bank Cash Mgt, Bank Bal. Rpt.)	$25,000	$20,000	$25,000	$23,000	$18,000	$28,000	$28,000	$25,000	

On closer examination, John saw that 3S stood for three states: the state of the customer, the state of the Value Stream, and the state of the company.

The form was tailored to his dad's airline, and it was interesting to note what they measured. John was just beginning to think about what measurements he would use to gauge the state of his group's customers, Value Stream, and company, when his phone rang.

"I just called to check that you got those charts," Tim said.

"I'm looking at the 3S Health Card right now," said John. "It's a pretty elaborate snapshot of the company. How often do you do this? Once a month . . . every quarter?"

"No, no. The 3S is a weekly report."

"You do this weekly? Doesn't that take a lot of time?" John looked at the figures, flabbergasted.

"No, my team sat down and came up with the most important measurements together. Your team will have to decide its own critical indicators. After you've got that, each team member is in charge of tracking one or two of these numbers every week, then we all review it together during our weekly Value Stream Performance Meeting. The weeks roll up to a monthly measurement.

"It's funny," said Tim, obviously thinking out loud, "usually it's just managers who get this type of information on the company's status, but it rarely comes in such a user-friendly format, with all the info on one page—at a glance, like this. Most times, it's scattered in a half-dozen reports that no one has time to sort through."

"I've never seen this kind of report at AXD," said John.

"Isn't that amazing?" asked Tim. "I've never understood how a team is supposed to make the right decisions for an organization from week to week without everyone having a clear picture of the three critical states of the business. And I've found that the more team members feel included in the measurement process, the more they take ownership of the results. You know, team members are hands down the best early-warning system for your company. They're up close to things, so they can spot problems in their infancy, before they become a complete disaster. Without them involved, many problem areas get overlooked."

Silently, John pictured the company as a patient hooked up to monitoring devices that no one ever checked. *By the time someone sees them, the patient might be critical—or worse,* he thought.

John looked up to see Todd passing his office and remembered how he used to compile the weekly report, which had been useless. *Maybe we could help pull the numbers we really need instead,* John thought. *Having Kiki involved might help draw her out a little, too.* After a moment, John realized that he and his dad had been sitting in silence, and he pulled his thoughts back to the second chart in front of him.

"What about this other report?" John asked. "The Financial Stream Sheet." (See report on the next page.)

"That's used to evaluate the flow of revenue by Value Stream and costs by major cost category. We use it to evaluate cost reduction as well as revenue and profit increase. It's essential in determining the financial health of a company."

John looked at it, realizing how much this information could help his group.

"How do you get these numbers?"

Revenue Streams	Week 1	Week 2	Week 3	Week 4	Total	Average	Last Month's Average	Last Month's Total	Revenue Increase
A	$700.00	$650.00	$900.00	$850.00	$3,100.00	$775.00	$650.00	$2,600.00	$500.00
B	$250.00	$450.00	$900.00	$750.00	$2,350.00	$587.50	$545.00	$2,180.00	$170.00
C	$1,000.00	$1,200.00	$900.00	$1,400.00	$4,500.00	$1,125.00	$1,200.00	$4,800.00	($300.00)
D	$1,500.00	$1,200.00	$1,600.00	$1,800.00	$6,100.00	$1,525.00	$1,300.00	$5,200.00	$900.00
TOTAL	$3,450.00	$3,500.00	$4,300.00	$4,800.00	$16,050.00	$4,012.50	$3,695.00	$14,780.00	$1,270.00

Cost Barriers	Week 1	Week 2	Week 3	Week 4	Total	Average	Last Month's Average	Last Month's Total	Cost Reduction
FUL	$750.00	$750.00	$750.00	$750.00	$3,000.00	$750.00	$800.00	$3,200.00	$200.00
VS Supplies	$2,500.00	$2,500.00	$2,500.00	$2,500.00	$10,000.00	$2,500.00	$2,800.00	$11,200.00	$1,200.00
Support	$250.00	$250.00	$250.00	$250.00	$1,000.00	$250.00	$350.00	$1,400.00	$400.00
COG	$200.00	$50.00	$0.00	$25.00	$275.00	$68.75	$200.00	$800.00	$525.00
TOTAL	$3,700.00	$3,550.00	$3,500.00	$3,525.00	$14,275.00	$3,568.75	$4,150.00	$16,600.00	$2,325.00

	Week 1	Week 2	Week 3	Week 4	Total	Average	Last Month's Average	Last Month's Total	Profit Increase
Revenue	$3,450.00	$3,500.00	$4,300.00	$4,800.00	$16,050.00	$4,012.50	$3,695.00	$14,780.00	
Cost	$3,700.00	$3,550.00	$3,500.00	$3,525.00	$14,275.00	$3,568.75	$4,150.00	$16,600.00	
Profit	($250.00)	($50.00)	$800.00	$1,275.00	$1,775.00	$443.75	($455.00)	-$1,820.00	$3,595.00

"That's where the Indirect Service Teams come into play," said Tim. "Planning and Analysis—or Accounting at AXD—should be able to support you by providing these numbers on a monthly basis. You'll need to talk to them and work it out."

In the background at his dad's house, John heard the screen door slam and his mom's voice.

"Well, I've got to go, Jack's stopped over to get beaten in chess again," Tim said. Again, the screen door slammed, and John heard a hearty laugh from the background. "Not this time, Tim," a man's voice replied.

John knew what to expect before it happened, and he braced himself for it: Without another word, his dad hung up.

CHAPTER 8

How Some Companies Just Keep Getting Better

The Secret of Kaizen

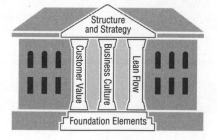

On Saturday, John woke late and padded to the door to retrieve his morning paper, rubbing his eyes. "Retailer on the Rocks . . . Again," the headline above the fold screamed, but John wasn't surprised.

The litany of the company's woes trailed across three pages, with executives deflecting the blame in all directions. The nationwide retailing giant had been in a slow decline for a long time, before finally going into bankruptcy reorganization last year. It had emerged from the proceedings with big plans and high hopes, but when John had stopped by the store a few months later, he'd found things just as bad as ever.

Slow cashiers. Employees who ran from you rather than help you. It was business as usual, with a few new aisles of merchandise, he remembered.

John lingered over breakfast and read the entire paper, all the while experiencing a vague feeling of guilt. The guilt was irrational, John had to remind himself. There was no looming crisis. For the first time in long time, things were going well at work; he could afford to relax a little.

Even measurement was moving along. With Kaye behind him, John had convinced accounting to provide the 3S report, which he expected to see for the first time on Monday. Mentec was happy, his team was working on the last module of code, and, unbelievably, they were one week ahead of schedule.

Kaye had dropped hints already about the team's next assignment; and John suspected it was the Glory Jeans account, another of the company's most significant clients.

Things couldn't be looking better, John thought happily. After a moment's deliberation, he made a decision. He was going golfing. He looked out the window at the sky. Not a cloud for miles. A perfect Saturday.

John was in midswing on the fourth hole when his cell phone rang. He ignored it; but his concentration was thrown off, and he ended up in the rough. Grumbling, he went after the ball. *I thought I turned that off*, he thought angrily, reaching into his pocket to retrieve the phone. He turned it off without checking for a message. *Whatever it is, can wait. Today, I'm on vacation.*

When he got home late in the afternoon, John felt relaxed. He emptied his keys and change from his pockets on the counter and plugged his phone into the charger. He was about to collapse on the couch when he remembered the call. Checking his messages, he was alarmed to find his mailbox full. All the calls were from his dad.

Was something wrong with Mom? John worried as he dialed the number.

His dad picked up on the first ring; and John could feel his heart pounding in his chest as he asked, "Is everything all right?"

"Sure," Tim answered. "I've been trying to find you all day. I must have called 20 times if I called once."

"Ten . . . no, eleven," corrected John, counting the messages. "Geez, you scared me. I thought something was wrong."

"Well, now that you mention it, something is," his dad replied. "But how would you know if you aren't looking for it?"

The response made no sense to John, and for a moment, he didn't know how to reply.

"Okay, Dad," he said finally. "Why don't you tell me why you called?"

"I wanted to talk about Kaizen," Tim said. "It's right about this time, when things are going well, that most leaders go on vacation."

John winced at the word vacation.

"They think they've fixed all the problems, and they relax and things start to slide. You got a moment?" Tim asked.

"I've got all the time you need," said John patiently. "But I don't have any problems."

"Leaders who say they have run out of seeds for improvement fall into one of three categories:

Either they don't notice current problems, or they can't foresee and predict problems, or they are content with the status quo and aren't motivated enough to raise their target.

"Look, I can guarantee there are problems within your process that you aren't seeing, because you're not actively looking for them," said Tim. "You need to implement Kaizen so you can see more clearly—and be motivated to improve."

With the phone in one hand, John picked up his golf bag and lugged it toward the closet. Of course, he remembered seeing Cultural Improvement on the roofline and wondering what it meant. So, it had meant Kaizen. He suddenly thought that perhaps he had been better off not knowing.

"Ignorance is bliss," said John, sighing.

"What?" his dad asked. When John didn't reply, Tim continued, "Kaizen is a never-ending change for the better. It's different from innovation, which is a dramatic, sudden, and inconsistent progress. You've seen companies like the one in the news today, that make really dramatic changes but haven't developed the culture to support them, so the innovations don't stick. In fact, they often become *Kaiaku*, which is change for the worse. Kaizen is slower and more consistent.

"I like to think of it this way: If innovation is an athlete jumping hurdles, going up and down, Kaizen is a mountain climber, moving consistently upward. It's slower, but you go higher."

John nodded, then temporarily tried to lodge the phone between his shoulder and ear. He caught it just before it hit the ground. Quickly putting it to his ear, he was relieved to find his dad hadn't noticed.

His dad was saying, ". . . so the first step is teaching team members to look for areas that are problems. You need perceptive people with an eye on cultural improvement. They should focus on work that needs improvement, quality problems, and awkward procedures that make work difficult.

"Some of these problems are easily identified, but others have to be predicted. Team members have to be able to discover future trends in present circumstances. This is called Preventative Kaizen. It's a little challenging, but the hardest problems to solve are the ones we create by applying a higher standard to our work. We create problems in a positive way by defining targets on a level that is higher than our present one," Tim was on a roll.

"One of the best ways to begin is to ask team members to recall improvements they have made in the past. That will trigger the right kind of thinking. Or try asking them to write things down that they aren't happy about."

"I'll try it on Monday, Dad," John agreed. "But, honestly, I've been racking my brain as you've been talking, and I can't think of a whole heap of outstanding problems right now."

"That's good, because it will keep you from making one of the most common mistakes of most leaders: Doing it yourself. A lot of coaches think they need to identify the problems themselves, as well as come up with the solutions, and *ensure* they are implemented. The whole process happens from the top down. But the truth is, you can't solve things effectively from the executive office. Kaizen has to start—and end—with team members.

"Well, I guess that's it for now," Tim said, a little regretfully. "How's your golf game?"

After hanging up, John stood a while in his living room staring into space. *So what are the problems that I'm not seeing at work?* Finally, he flopped down onto the couch intending to take his nap. But somehow he didn't feel much like sleeping anymore.

What are the problems that I'm not seeing at work?

Monday morning's staff meeting was unusual, to say the least. John introduced the topic of past improvements, which instantly launched the group into a heated discussion about the wisdom of past technology choices. John found it hard to bring the conversation around, but was rewarded for his efforts when Kiki spoke up.

"I've always wondered about our standards for documentation. We each do it differently, and, well," Kiki had floundered here, as she registered all eyes on her. "Well. . . ."

Kiki seemed unable to continue. She looked down at her hands in her lap. To John's surprise, it was Ray who jumped to her assistance.

"Kiki's brought this up a few times with me. I guess I've never bothered much about it because everything was such a mess before, and documentation seemed like the least of our worries. But now that things are under control," Ray looked briefly at John, then quickly away. "Well, now might be a good time to look at that."

John quickly wrote it down. It made him remember something his dad had said recently: "A problem is a deviation from a standard; therefore, standardization sets the stage for improvement. Many people feel they have a problem when they really have chaos, because there is no standard to define what the problem is. Where's there's no standard, there's no Kaizen."

Documentation would give them a standard, a place for improvement to begin, he thought.

"Another thing is the slowness of the latest module. I don't think it will bother Mentec, at least not at first. But there has to be a better way to do it," said Blake.

"And I'm getting an error message in the latest module, and I can't seem to pinpoint the cause," said Ray.

John wrote down each of these problems, with a feeling that he was checking things off on a list. After a brief, unproductive discussion about the error message, he turned the time over to Blake to update the team on Mentec.

The rest of the week went by quickly, and John rarely thought about the Kaizen list until Friday, when he returned to his office to find an overnight package on his desk.

As he opened it, a small, homemade book fell out. Flipping through it, he recognized his dad's furious handwriting and his mom's quick line drawings. Obviously, it wasn't a project that had occupied much of their time, but it was fascinating. He turned to page one and began to read:

> Not long ago, the leader of a large bakery called his mechanical engineers together and gave them a critical assignment. For years, all the steps in the pasty-making process had been automated except for a tiny knot of dough that sealed in the filling. The knot had to be created by hand, which slowed production dramatically.
>
> "To survive, we must automate the knot," said the president. The engineers were at first, overwhelmed by the challenge, but after many sleepless nights and months of research and development, they succeeded in their task.
>
> The president was overjoyed to hear this and called the company together to celebrate. But in the midst of the

resulting noise and confusion, someone on the production line quietly asked, "What is the knot for, anyway?"

The factory fell quiet. No one had ever asked this question. In their fervor to solve the problem, no one, from the president to the engineers, had considered why the knot existed in the first place.

Finally, an elderly woman, the oldest worker at the plant, stepped forward. She remembered that, back when the plant used to make many kinds of pastries, the knot was used to distinguish between the different fillings inside. However, since the factory now only used one type of filling, the knot no longer served any practical purpose.

Instantly, the mood within the factory turned sober as each person came to the same realization: Rather than being automated, the knot should have been eliminated.

John turned to the last page and read,

The moral of the story: Before you tie up your resources, be certain you fully understand the problem at hand.

Are you sure you fully understand your problem?

The last line was written in red ink, and John reread it several times, thinking about each of their three Kaizens and what the purpose of each might be.

What was the purpose of documentation? It was supposed to help guide programmers who took over the code maintenance. But since his group was going to maintain the code, John wondered how important it really would be. He didn't have to wonder long.

He looked up and found Kiki standing in front of his desk. She smiled and said, apologetically, "I knocked, but you didn't hear."

He motioned for her to sit down and waited for her to speak.

"Umm, I wanted to tell you as far in advance as I could," she said, sitting on the edge of her chair and leaning forward. "I'm going to be leaving AXD. My husband has accepted a job in Phoenix, and we'll be moving in three weeks."

"Three weeks!" John was shocked. Instantly, his mind reviewed the time frame. The final code was due in two weeks, and with this error message making things difficult. . . .

"The company wanted Chris immediately, but I insisted on having enough time to wrap up our project before I left. I wouldn't leave if this weren't such a great opportunity for him."

As Kiki spoke, John suddenly realized the urgency of documentation. Someone would have to be brought in to take over Kiki's duties, and that someone would have to come up to speed very quickly on the code already written. They needed something effective and clear, but not overly complex.

"You're not angry, are you?" asked Kiki nervously.

John realized with a start that he had been lost in thought. "No, of course not, Kiki. I'm just wondering how we'll ever get along without you. You've been such a great asset to the group."

Kiki beamed. "Then I can use you as a reference?" she asked.

When Kiki left the room following a quick discussion of her future plans, John looked down at the hand-drawn book. It was lying face down, and John noticed writing on the back he'd overlooked before.

"If the purpose of a job is not made clear, people focus too much on the means of doing it. They forget there might be more than one way to get the end result."

Well, the purpose of documentation is suddenly abundantly clear, thought John. *The goal is to transfer knowledge. Now, we've just got to find the right way to get it done.* He picked up the phone to call a meeting.

That night, John stayed at the office long after everyone had gone home. Just before leaving, he picked up the phone to call his dad.

"Got your book. I think it's going to be a best seller."

"Nah," said his dad. "Nothing like that. Just a lighthearted way to make a point."

"We had a good meeting about Kaizen today. Once we clearly identified the purpose of documentation, it was easier to choose a way forward."

"Oh, yeah? It's easy to get stuck in a loop and never get out of the idea phase. Some people think the mental gymnastics of the creative thinking process are enough. But the ability to select and implement solutions is critical. Kaizen is only valuable when implemented."

Kaizen is only valuable when implemented.

John agreed. "Well, once Ray realized that documentation wasn't just an academic exercise—that it had a real and pressing purpose—we were able to start making some of those decisions. I think he had gotten into the mode of thinking of documentation as the purpose, instead of the real rationale of transferring knowledge."

"You know, it reminds me of that park we used to take you to when you were little," said Tim. "There was this little old man who was there every day sweeping up garbage. He worked for the city. One day I asked him why they didn't put more garbage cans out, so people could more easily clean up their own trash, and he said that then he'd be out of a job. He'd missed the whole point. To him, the job of cleaning had become the purpose, not a clean park."

John had to laugh. "Yep," he said. "Been there. But we're moving forward now that we're straight on the purpose. We've decided on a standard, and we're offering Kiki some overtime to make sure her code is documented before she leaves. And then we're retaining her as an on-call consultant."

"Kiki's leaving?"

"She turned in her notice today."

His dad groaned a little, sympathetically. John went on. "But we've got a couple of other problems right now: Ray keeps saying the new module has an error that we can't weed out. And it runs too slowly. Any ideas?"

Tim laughed. "Do you have to ask? When have I not had something to say? Actually, there are three courses to take once you've identified the purpose of Kaizen. Basically, you can: eliminate, reduce, or change."

"Okay," said John, waiting for an explanation.

"Well, it's natural to come up with another activity to improve the original one, but this ignores the basic principle of elimination. Before considering other activities, consider whether you can drop the activity altogether. Ask yourself, 'What will happen if this is eliminated?' If the answer is 'nothing' or even 'not much,' then you've just found the most effective and inexpensive solution possible. Elimination is the ultimate Kaizen."

"Well, that's not an option here," said John. "This module is required."

"Okay, then consider reduction. Why not ask Ray to go through the code again, this time with the mindset that he will identify the purpose of every line of code and eliminate any that are not absolutely essential."

John thought for a moment. "Now, that might work," he said. "We'll try it. It might help with the speed problem, too."

"Possibly. But if it doesn't—and you can't eliminate or reduce—try changing. Not the entire module, but consider changing some elements of it."

It took Ray a whole day to walk through the code. John had a lot to do, but his mind kept returning to Ray and hoping that the review turned up something.

At the end of the day, Ray knocked on his door.

"Found it," he said, exuberantly.

"You did? You found the cause of the error message?"

"It was a duplicate line of code in exactly the wrong place. It put the code into a continuous loop. I took that line out, and the problem was solved."

"Does the module run faster?"

"No, it didn't help with that, but the code is cleaner, now. And it runs right. And I documented as I went."

"Well, sounds like a good day's work. Excellent, Ray. Really well done."

Two down and one to go, thought John to himself at the end of the day as he threw some paperwork into his briefcase. He would have to hurry or the dry cleaners would be closed.

As he walked into the small shop, the woman behind the counter looked up and smiled. "Hi, John."

John loved how pleasant the people at the dry cleaners were. As he showed the woman the small tear near the seam on the shoulder, she laughed. "It seems like you'd save a lot of money on shirt repairs if you'd just fix that nail in the door. You know, prevention is the best repair."

John laughingly agreed. But it made him think. Every shirt he had torn *had* caught on his office door. He'd never made the connection before; but now it made perfect sense: There must be a nail that needed to be removed. Why hadn't he thought about it before he'd ruined this second shirt?

He paid in advance and left with his ticket clutched in his hand.

"I jumped too far ahead. I got focused on fixing the shirts and forgot to figure out what was causing them to be torn. I wonder . . ."

An idea was forming in his mind. Maybe, just maybe, that was the same mistake they were making with the slow software. "We've jumped into solving the problem without really examining the root cause."

He pulled out his Palm Pilot and made an entry for another team meeting, first thing in the morning. After a moment's thought, he added another notation, reminding himself to bring in a hammer.

John got to work early and quickly pulled a tiny but sharp finishing nail from his door frame.

"Gotcha!" he said, triumphantly.

On his way to pick up a cup of coffee, he passed the fax machine, where he noticed a cover sheet bearing his name.

He picked it up and discovered a list of things to look for in hiring people.

"This is my guide for hiring," his dad had scribbled in the margin. John took a closer look at the paper labeled with an acronym—POEM-T:

This is my guide for hiring.

POEM-T

Positive
Do they give off a positive energy and seem to have an overall positive outlook?

Obedience
Are they willing to follow instructions consistently?

Endurance
What is the toughest thing they have come through, and how did they come through it?

Motivation
Do they have internal passion that is heartfelt, deep and authentic, and that makes them excited about work?

Transparent
Do they volunteer information? Look for honesty and integrity as you interview them.

Looking at it, John realized how far his team had come. Just a few weeks ago, he might not have considered hiring any of them, certainly not if he had been using this standard.

Still, something about each of them had persuaded a manager to hire them. *Had Ray started out as positive and strong and motivated—even eager?* he wondered. And, like him, were they now rediscovering qualities that had been buried for a long, long time?

It was then that John noticed several additional sheets of paper still lying on the fax machine. It looked like a report.

"7K," John read out loud. Scanning through the pages, his eyes widened in surprise. "Just like being led to the Wizard of Oz, only to find out the solution was in you all along. Still you have to follow the right path to get there," he said to himself. The thought made him smile; and as he walked toward the break room, he couldn't keep from whistling one verse of "Follow the Yellow Brick Road":

VALUE-CENTERED ENTERPRISE
7K Report
Page 1 of 3

VALUE STREAM NAME: <u>YOUR VALUE STREAM NAME</u>   DATE: TODAY'S DATE

STEP 1: IDENTIFY OPPORTUNITY AND SELECT KAIZEN GOAL

A. Opportunity Statement
This is a brief statement that outlines what the standard is numerically, and how it has been deviated from. It is important to explain this numerically to clearly see the opportunity for improvement.

B. Brief Background and History
Provide background information to explain what the standard is. Has the standard been met in the past?

C. Opportunity Evaluation

Importance/Urgency: *Why is it so important or urgent to resolve this problem?*

Affected Parties: *What specific Value Streams people, teams, work cells, etc. does this affect?*

Desired Resolution Timeframe: ☐ Within 1 Week   ☐ Within 1 Month   ☐ Within 3 Months
☐ Within 6 Months   ☐ Within 9 Months   ☐ Within 1 Year

Scope of Control: *How much control do you have in implementing a kaizen for this particular opportunity?*

D. Consequence(s) of this Problem
What are the current effects of the problem on the Value Stream?

E. Kaizen Statement
Write a statement outlining the Kaizen goal. Be sure to make it a measurable (numerical) goal so it is clear to measure whether or not it is being reached.

STEP 2: ANALYZE THE PROBLEM

Brainstorm Potential Causes: List each "cause category" first.

CAUSE CATEGORY	CAUSE CATEGORY	
Potential Cause	Potential Cause	**OPPORTUNITY STATEMENT**
Potential Cause	Potential Cause	
Potential Cause	Potential Cause	*Write the opportunity statement here.*
Potential Cause	Potential Cause	
Potential Cause	Potential Cause	
Potential Cause	Potential Cause	
CAUSE CATEGORY	CAUSE CATEGORY	

Determine Main Cause: *Write the best potential cause here.*

5 Why Analysis	Investigation/Answer
Why: *Form a "why" question to find out information about the potential cause.*	*Explain how you investigated to answer this "why" question.*
Why: *Form another "why" question to gather more specific information.*	*Explain how you investigated to answer this "why" question.*
Why: *Form another "why" question to gather more specific information.*	*Explain how you investigated to answer this "why" question.*
Why: *Form another "why" question to gather more specific information.*	*Explain how you investigated to answer this "why" question.*
Why: *Form another "why" question to gather more specific information. Ask as many questions as needed to find the root cause of the problem.*	*Explain how you investigated to answer this "why" question.*

WHY WHY WHY WHY

Root Cause
Write the root cause statement here.

STEP 3: ANALYZE POTENTIAL KAIZENS

ROOT CAUSE: *Write the root cause statement here.*

Potential Kaizens	Scope of Control	Relevance	Minimal Resources	Expected Results	Buy In	Total Score
Scope of Control: *How much control do you have to implement this Kaizen?* **Relevance:** *How relevant is this Kaizen to actually solving the problem?* **Minimal Resources:** *Can you use minimal resources (people, money, time) to implement this Kaizen?* **Expected Results:** *How strong will the results of this Kaizen be?* **Buy In:** *How likely is it that the affected parties will cooperate in implementing this Kaizen?*						
Rate each category from 1 - 5 (Lowest - Highest)						
1. *Write potential Kaizen ideas*						
2. *Write potential Kaizen ideas*						
3. *Write potential Kaizen ideas*						
4. *Write potential Kaizen ideas*						
5. *Write potential Kaizen ideas*						

VALUE-CENTERED ENTERPRISE
7K Report
Page 3 of 3

STEP 4: SELECT THE BEST KAIZEN
Write the highest scoring Kaizen idea here. In the case of a tied score, you will have to analyze further to determine what the best Kaizen idea is.

STEP 5: KAIZEN IMPLEMENTATION PLAN		
What	Who	When
What exact steps are required to fully implement this Kaizen? Be sure to include your planned evaluation dates after implementation.	*Who is responsible for completing each step?*	*When will each step be completed? Give an exact date.*

STEP 6: EVALUATE KAIZEN EFFECTIVENESS	
Observation Date	Comments about Results
Date of observation	*What results were obtained? Be sure to write this numerically in comparison with the opportunity statement.*

STEP 7: SUBMIT KAIZEN FORM
SUBMITTED KAIZEN FORM ON: <u>WRITE THE DATE YOUR KAIZEN FORM WAS SUBMITTED</u>

John began the staff meeting by handing out blank copies of the 7K Report. His team members eyed the report doubtfully.

"Oh, come on. Give it a chance. We're here to figure out why the latest module runs too slowly," said John. "This form can help us. First we have to come up with an opportunity statement, which means we need to identify the problem."

"I thought you just did," said Kiki. "The module runs too slowly."

"It's got to be more specific than that and measurable," said John. "How slowly is it running? How

much time do we need to shave off it? We need to figure out the standard and how far we've deviated
from it."

"Well, this module has a cycle time of 45 seconds,
and our standard cycle time is 5 seconds," said Ray in
a resigned tone.

He's not buying this, thought John, *but he knows
he's obligated to go through it.*

John continued moving the group through the
form. Together, they identified a Kaizen statement.

"Our Kaizen goal is to reduce the module's cycle
time from 45 seconds to 5," said Kiki, catching the
spirit of the report.

Next, the group spent 30 minutes listing possible
causes using a fishbone diagram. The brainstorming
process seemed to bring them out a little more. Looking at the list at the end of the time, one cause seemed
the most likely: a problem with the database.

By the time they got to the 5 Why Analysis, John
was starting to enjoy the process. He liked the way
the report led them logically from one step to the
other, but it proved to be the wrong time to let down
his guard.

"Darn it!" Ray pounded the table in frustration
after John had asked "Why?" for the fifth time. "I already told you why: I don't know!" Kiki stood frozen
at the whiteboard, where she was writing down their
responses.

"Look, I'm sorry, but I'm asking why to allow us to
probe deeper into the reasons behind the problem,"
said John, who was beginning to question the process himself. *Why was this so hard?* When his dad
had explained it last night, the process had seemed
so logical.

"Every time you come up with a reason for the
problem, ask why the reason exists," Tim had ex-

plained. "If someone says the reason is because you're using a different software, ask why you are using a different software. If they say it's because nothing else worked, ask why it didn't work. You have to ask the question at least five times to get to the root cause—and sometimes even more. It's like digging for buried treasure. You've got to remove a lot of worthless layers to reveal the gold beneath."

Unfortunately, in practice they seemed to have hit a barrier.

"Wait, I know," said Kiki, interrupting John's thoughts. "Remember? We didn't want to apply for permission to access the legacy database because we figured it would be too much of a hassle. We figured we could write around it."

"Yeah, I guess that seems right," Blake said. "We planned this all out so long ago, I'd forgotten. But we designed this module as a workaround. Maybe the workaround isn't working."

"So, if we could get access to that database," said John, slowly, "you're saying we could design this module using the same model as the others that run more quickly?"

"Yes!" Kiki, Ray, and Blake all said together, suddenly exuberant.

Energized by their success in identifying the problem's root cause, the group moved on to analyzing potential Kaizens. However, it quickly became clear why they had originally chosen a workaround. Securing access to the database would not be easy. There was a lot of red tape involved—and one very difficult personality. Len in Processing was a bear to deal with.

At the end of the discussion, John looked down at the words he had written for Step 4: John will formally request access from Len in the Processing Group. He gulped. He knew it was the best solution. It had scored the highest on the chart, and had the best scope of control, relevance, expected results, and a minimal outlay of resources. Not surprisingly, it also got a lot of buy-in from the group, mostly because he would be the one to approach Len.

"Okay, I'll do it," said John. "But we're going to need a plan. What do we need to do first? Talk to Kaye? Take the Processing Group to lunch? Maybe it would be easier if we all just picked up and moved to Aruba. I'll foot the bill."

Everyone laughed, but John still wasn't sure he hadn't been completely serious.

Leaving the meeting that afternoon, everyone had an assignment. Kiki and Todd would finish up an assignment Len had asked them to take care of long ago, which had been put on the back burner. Ray would begin designing the new module. All of it would culminate in John's call on Friday.

The success of their Kaizen's effectiveness would be clear within one week, when they tested the revised module. Thinking about the progress the team had made, John felt optimistic. Maybe he wouldn't have to start pricing airfare to the islands after all.

That night, John still felt like celebrating. He dressed quickly for the theater with Stephanie, something he might usually try to avoid. He grabbed the wrapped box, her surprise gift, and picked up his keys. But, on his way to the door, he stopped dead in his tracks, transfixed. Something was different about his prized abstract painting on the wall. No, something was different about *him.*

For some reason, looking at the blue waves, he was filled with the same energy he'd felt the day he'd bought the painting, the same day he'd been hired. John drank in the feeling of excitement and anticipation that had been missing for so long.

I'm feeling brand new, he realized. *We're two weeks from our deadline and ahead of schedule. Mentec is thrilled—and I'm feeling excited about work again.*

Kaizen is changing things, he thought. *And definitely for the better.*

EPILOGUE

Four weeks later, John was seated in the Thai Café with Stephanie and his parents, glasses raised in a toast.

"To Dad," said John, proudly, "who saved my career and my sanity."

"To John," said Tim, beaming, "who had the guts to take a chance on something unknown."

The waitress arrived with the food. She noticed the smiling faces around the table and the raised glasses.

"Is this a special occasion?" she asked.

"My son just got a promotion," said Tim. "He's the new director of Value-Centered Management for AXD Software."

John flushed a little as the waitress looked his way and offered her congratulations and another round of drinks, on the house.

For John, the last week had been a blur of meetings, first with Kaye, and then, as the word got out on the success of the Mentec project, in a presentation to the entire management committee.

Then, two days ago, instead receiving the name of the new project he had been anticipating, he had been called into his VP's office, where he found Kaye and the CEO waiting.

"This company has been around a long time," the CEO warned. "We'll have to take this one step at a time. But you've done something here that is truly remarkable. We've tried a lot of management fads around here over the years, most of them largely ineffective. But you've proven that Value-Centered Management can work. We think it could benefit the entire corporation. And we want you to lead the transformation."

As the CEO spoke, John kept his eyes fixed on his face, afraid to catch Kaye's eye. He was afraid she would feel angry at his rapid rise to a corporate position almost equal her own. But, when he finally dared look her way, he found a strange look of relief on her face.

After the CEO left for another meeting, she stood to shake John's hand. As they walked to the door, she leaned close and whispered. "I knew you were on your way up when we met in your office a few weeks ago," she said. "I just prayed you weren't going to displace me along the way."

But none of it seemed real until the day the movers hung his blue painting on his new office wall. It looked at home there, like it had always been meant to hang there. John, however, felt less at ease. After the movers filed out, John stood for a moment, wondering where to begin. *There's so much more to learn, and I have so many questions: How do I hire the right team to implement Value-Centered Management, create a Value-Centered strategy, define leadership levels from a Value-Centered perspective, implement the methodology in diverse departmental environments, utilize the tools that I've learned in greater detail, teach team members this management approach in a standard way that is easy to understand, and so on? I don't know where to begin.* It was an awkward feeling, standing on the edge of something new and uncharted.

As he moved forward to straighten the picture, he heard the fax machine begin to whir; and he noticed a message coming through. John smiled as he read it. The words were simple: "You have a new job. Now go look, go see. You have to observe the current situation before you can act. You know what to do. You've done this before. Don't rest on your laurels. Get into gear."

Dad was right. It wasn't that long ago that he'd been here before, on the edge of something unknown, going toe-to-toe with tradition. He could still hear his dad's passionate voice asking, "Who said so? Who said the way it's always been done is the only way? Who said there isn't a better way to do things?" The words had motivated him to begin his first experimentation with Value-Centered Management.

What—and where—would this new step bring him?

John couldn't wait to find out. With his father's words still ringing in his ears, he put down the paper and stepped out his office door into a future of endless possibility.

VALUE-CENTERED MANAGEMENT GLOSSARY

3S Health Card A weekly value-centered tool to measure three critical states of the business: the state of the customer, value stream, and organization.

5 Why Analysis A method to get to the root cause of a problem by asking "why" of a problem at least five times. (You may have to ask more or less than five times.)

Accounting Service Team A service team responsible for accounting for the money coming into the organization and the money going out of the organization on a day-to-day basis.

Batch A batch consists of large quantities of items moving through the process, which causes queue times or waiting. It is desirable to have a one-piece flow versus a batch system.

Buffer A type of safety stock often necessary to ensure you consistently meet customer demand when customer ordering patterns or customer pace times vary.

Built-in Quality Build quality into the process in such a way that prevents mistakes, defects, or breaking of standards. Equipment or processes that are set up to make it easy to discover abnormalities.

Business Health The soundness and vitality of the enterprise, which can be measured by keeping an accurate understanding of the state of the customer, state of the value stream, and the state of the company.

Business Support Cost   The cost associated with activities that indirectly support the business's ability to serve the customer.

Continuous Flow   Setting up processes so that a product or service can flow through the operation in the proper sequence and without interruptions due to imbalances.

Cost Barriers   Any cost associated with business is considered a barrier that should be reduced or removed in the value-centered enterprise.

Cost of Goods to be Sold   The cost associated with purchasing inventory that will be sold to earn revenue.

Cost Reduction   A foundational element of value-centered management. This principle deals with the main four types of business related costs: F.U.L. cost, inventory and materials cost, business support cost, and cost of goods to be sold. The reduction of all these costs is essential to maximizing the profit of the value-centered enterprise.

Cost Reduction Principle   Sales price minus cost equals profit. Sales price is decided according to market conditions. Profit is increased only if costs are reduced, not by increasing the sales price.

Culture   A healthy environment for the team members who serve our customers. Company culture is the heart of the Value-Centered Enterprise.

Cultural Improvement Systems   A system that allows the company culture to be controlled by team members who have been trained how to see and implement improvement.

Cultural Ingredients Key ingredients in a Value-Centered Enterprise: cultural improvement systems, leadership development, team member development, and customer service.

Customer Anyone who is in receipt of, or desires to receive, a service or product and is willing to pay for it.

Customer Demand What we need to produce on a daily basis to satisfy the customers we serve.

Customer Pace Time The pace at which the operation must move to ensure it meets the demand of its customers. Customer demand divided by planned work time equals customer pace time.

Customer Service In the value-centered enterprise, customer service must go deeper than a smile. We must understand what our customers value, then take the time to center all operations, policies, procedures, and behaviors around that value.

Customer Value Committee A committee of dedicated customers used to gather information and feedback on the products and services currently offered and/or future products, services, or strategies being considered by the company.

Customer Value Alignment Chart A tool to match identified value points from the customer to specific processes within the value stream or operation to seek improvement from the customer's perspective.

Direct Service Team The service teams directly associated with delivering the products and/or services for which the business was created.

FIFO First In, First out; a method for work-control so that older work (first in) is the first to be processed (first out).

Flow A sequence of activities or processes necessary to deliver a product or service to the customer.

F.U.L. Cost The cost associated with having the facilities, utilities, and labor necessary to run your business.

Go-Gos Go see, go touch, go smell, go taste, and/ or go hear for yourself what is actually happening when trying to grasp a problem or validate an improvement. Do not settle for what someone else has told you.

Heijunka A Japanese term meaning "level scheduling" or "smoothing" to ensure a balanced workload and balanced production of goods or providing of services to the customer. A physical device used to level work volume and variety over a specified period.

Human Resources Service Team Service team responsible for working with value-stream leadership to facilitate the activities surrounding how people enter the company, work within the company, and exit the company.

Indirect Service Teams The service teams that indirectly serve the customer by providing support services to the Direct-Service Teams and company as a whole. There are seven main indirect service teams in the Value-Centered Enterprise: value management, partnership management, accounting, human resources, information and technology, planning and analysis, and the kaizen service team.

Information Technology Service Team Service team responsible for managing the company's ability to move, locate, and store the information necessary to ensure the company can fulfill its mission of consistent creation and delivery of value.

Inventory Materials, parts, or information needed to provide a product or service to a customer.

Jidoka Building intelligence into equipment or processes that allow problems to be visible so they can be detected and resolved on the spot (e.g., an electronic form that cannot be sent until all fields are completed).

Just-in-Time (JIT) Only producing what is needed, just when it is needed, in the exact amount needed and in the right quantity.

Kaizen Continuous change for the better. Kai = change, Zen = for the better.

Kaizen Service Team Service team responsible for managing cultural improvement systems throughout the company to ensure the kaizen spirit never dies, and that successful kaizens are shared to the benefit of the entire enterprise.

Kanban Inventory control card used to manage inventory in a lean environment, which focuses on minimizing inventory and only moving inventory at the pace of customer demand (pull system).

Lean A manufacturing method/system founded by the Toyota Production System based on the goal of eliminating waste to maximize value to the customer.

Lean Accounting Financial accounting approach necessary in a lean environment to ensure the benefits of lean management are realized financially, while also eliminating many wastes that are present in traditional financial accounting.

Leveling Distributing work evenly to enhance and create a productive work flow that ensures all work within an operation is balanced, so that no process or person is overworked or strained, and flow can be enhanced.

Line Balancing   The process of evenly distributing work elements within a value stream in order to meet takt time and ensure a proper workload balance for your team members.

Muda   A Japanese term meaning "waste" or "nonvalue-added."

Nonvalue-Added Demand   Abnormal demands from the client due to inefficiencies or failures within the value stream.

Pitch   A multiple of takt time that will allow you to customize your takt time requirement into a manageable goal for a particular work flow, process, or value stream.

Pitch Board   A visual control method that will assist in controlling the flow of work throughout the workday by displaying visually how the process is flowing with respect to takt time.

Planned Work Time   Actual time allotted for actual work to be done. You must subtract lunches, breaks, and so on to calculate this time.

Planning and Analysis Service Team   Service team responsible for the coordination and fulfillment of the planning and analysis necessary to ensure the organization is prepared for short- and long-term success.

Point-to-Point (PTP) Time   The total time it takes to get from one point to another within an operation, or from the beginning to the end of an operation or sequence of activities.

Principles of Lean   Key lean principles include: cost reduction principle, lead-time reduction, customer service, respect for team members, eight deadly wastes, just-in-time, built-in quality, three phases of lean application, the visual office, and kaizen environment.

Principles of Value-Centered Management The principal topics and methodologies relating to Value-Centered Management Fundamentals, Understanding Value, Understanding Culture, Understanding Flow, and Structure and Strategy.

Process Time   Time it takes to perform or operate a process one time.

Process Time Percentage The percent of the point-to-point time spent actually working. Process time divided by the point-to-point time.

Pull System   Only producing what is requested by the next process (or downstream process) or customer (internal or external), thus minimizing inventory since everything is done based on a response to an actual need expressed by the customer.

Push System   Production with no regard for what is needed by your customer or by the next process. Work piles up in batches and is pushed from process to process, normally creating excessive amounts of inventory.

Relative Wait Time Percentage   The relationship between the process and wait time.

Revenue Streams   Every product or service that can be sold to produce revenue for the company.

SAFE-T is an acronym coined by Value-Centered Management. SAFE-T certified environments are safe, clean, and orderly.

1. **Separate** what is needed from those items that are not needed for your current operation (bare essentials).

2. **Arrange** all needed items in a permanent home in your environment with strategic consideration of interior design, ergonomics, and frequency of use.

3. **Finish** by keeping everything swept and clean. It emphasizes the removal of dirt, grime, and dust from all items in the environment.

4. **Everyone** creates a consistent way that tasks and procedures are carried out through the use of pictures, labels, and other visual controls.

5. **Test** by making a habit of properly maintaining correct procedures through daily/weekly checklists and auditing systems.

Safety Stock Extra inventory, time, and/or resources used as a means of meeting customer demand when internal constraints, external constraints, or inefficiencies endanger the normal process flow.

Scorecard A lean tool used to measure productivity and performance of a value stream on a regular basis.

Service Team A team member or group of team members who are responsible for a process(es) to support the value stream. There are two types of service teams: direct and indirect.

Seven Commitments Value-Centered Management teaches that there are seven key commitments that everyone in the organization must focus on at all times. These commitments cannot be compromised but must be promoted, celebrated, and adhered to. They are:

1. **Attitude control:** All team members must commit to controlling their attitude and demonstrate their ability to manage their own behavior.

2. **Identifying and strengthening individual weaknesses:** The strength of the team members within an organization lies in their ability to identify and strengthen their individual weaknesses and commit to work on them constantly.

3. **Positive thought process:** It is critical that team members commit to having a positive thought process, no matter the business circumstance. Before any team can act right, they must first think right.

4. **Effective communication:** All team members must commit to sending effective messages and being willing to receive messages from others through active listening to ensure effective communication.

5. **High tolerance level:** All team members must commit to having a high tolerance level for dealing with challenges that may come up within the course of the operation of the business.

6. **Resilience:** All team members must commit to learning how to recover when they are feeling down or upset. No matter what we do, there are going to be things that happen that frustrate us; however, we must commit to bounce back quickly.

7. **Respect for authority:** All team members must commit to respecting the authority given to diverse individuals within the organization. Without an environment in which respect is promoted and honored among team members, customers will not receive the proper respect they deserve.

Seven Nonvalue-Added Activities In the value-centered enterprise we focus on maximizing value-added activity. This is also consistent with focusing on minimizing nonvalue-added activity. There are seven nonvalue-added activities, which should be continually, intensely focused on and eliminated:

1. **Overproviding:** Providing more product, work, time, and/or serving than is necessary to serve your customer.

2. **Unnecessary waiting:** There is no value added when customers or team members are waiting for something or someone.

3. **Unnecessary quantities:** Having a higher quantity of items or information than necessary to do the job required in the operation.

4. **Unnecessary movement:** The unnecessary movement of items, people, or a person within an operation or process.

5. **Repeat work:** Having to do something over again because it was not done right the first time.

6. **Irrelevant work:** Doing things within an operation that are irrelevant to the customer.

7. **Underutilized resources:** A person or machine that is not being fully used to their potential to provide value to the client.

Stream The flow of activities and processes that move the products and/or service from the company to the client.

Supermarket A system used to store a set level of completed work units or partially completed work units (WIP) to ensure the demands of the next process or customer can be properly met. The supermarket is only replenished based on a pull from the next process or customer.

Takt Time   The pace of customer demand, calculated by dividing the net available operating time by the total daily quantity required to meet customer demand.

Time Management   A foundation element of value-centered management. Time management refers to understanding the different time elements associated with servicing the customer, such as process time, wait time and point-to-point time. There are also three important time management percentages: process time percentage, wait time percentage, and relative wait time percentage. One of the most important elements of time management is understanding the customer pace time.

Toyota Production System   The original name for lean management, which is Toyota's management and production philosophy developed in the mid-twentieth century.

Value   The innermost driving force that would cause a person to spend their money to buy a product or service.

Value Added   All activities that are essential to producing value for the customer.

Value-Added Demand   The normal demand associated with the customer's request to be serviced by the value stream.

Value-Centered Enterprise   Any enterprise that has mastered the ability to center all of its operations around what the customer values consistently over time, while maintaining the necessary culture to sustain the smooth, productive flow of value to customers.

Value-Centered Management   A management approach that completely centers itself around what the customer values, by focusing on consistent value creation and flow in a focused and team member friendly culture.

Value-Centered Management Fundamentals The foundation elements of Value-Centered Management. The key fundamentals are a visual workplace, time management, cost reduction, reduction of nonvalue-added activities, and resource reallocation.

Value Focus Groups A focus group of customers of one's business used to gather information about their specific values and provide advice about customer-focused company direction.

Value-Management Service Team Service team within the value-centered enterprise that focuses on continually identifying and maintaining what the customer values and ensures these values are being properly incorporated into all service teams within the value stream.

Value Stream The stream of activities and or processes grouped within service teams to deliver the products and/or services that the customer values.

Value Stream Mapping Visual mapping tool developed to understand the workplace and to identify value- and nonvalue-added activities within an operation or value stream.

Visual Control Visual-management techniques that express information in a way that can be understood quickly by everyone and assist in controlling the flow of work and communicating workplace standards.

Visual Workplace A foundation element of Value-Centered Management. A workplace that is equipped with visual management tools such as pictures, labels, posters, checklists, and visual standards to remind everyone of the rules for the operation and to track job progress.

Waste A lean-manufacturing term used to describe anything that adds time or cost without adding value.

Wait Time The amount of time a product or customer waits to be processed or serviced.

Wait-Time Percentage The percentage of point-to-point time spent waiting between processes. Wait time divided by point-to-point time.

Work-Balance Chart A visual display of the work elements, times, and team members at each location, used for the purpose of ensuring a proper work balance for an operation.

Work Cell A group of team members who have commonalities in terms of equipment and processing systems, causing them to work in a specific location as a team to fulfill a particular function or process within a value stream.

Work in Progress Work that was not completed in a given day or time period, and is still being processed somewhere within the operation or value stream.

Workplace Management A management system used to implement and sustain a lean, orderly, and safe environment in all workplaces throughout the value stream.

ABOUT THE AUTHOR

Michael Parker is president and CEO of Stellar Enterprise, a nationwide organization thriving within a unique business paradigm. By marrying lean practices—once restricted to the manufacturing industry—to a focus on creating real value in customers' minds, Mr. Parker has achieved authentic corporate nirvana: customer satisfaction ratings of more than 90 percent and annual revenue growth of 25 percent.

His success began with a question: Who Said So?

As a professional charged with implementing lean principles throughout Toyota North America operations, Mr. Parker wondered if lean would work equally well in other industries. The question gave rise to other questions, such as, "Are what customers say they want and what customers truly value the same things?" Such atypical questions led his fledgling organization on its path toward achieving out-of-the-ordinary results.

In *Who Said So?* Mr. Parker brings together a rich background in lean manufacturing with a passion for researching and understanding what creates real value in customers' minds. The discussion is guided by questions that rock business traditions—and make organizations and their leaders stronger.

To get a closer, more in-depth view of the principles and tools that make up this revolutionary approach to business, visit vcminstitute.com. There, you can learn more about our seminars, consultants, and tap into resources that can assist in building a profitable, vibrant Value-Centered Organization in any business environment.

In addition, Michael holds an MBA in management science from Cal State University Hayward, where he is an instructor on Lean Management and Just-in-Time Systems.